THE POWER OF COMMUNICATION SKILLS AND EFFECTIVE LISTENING

SAY WHAT YOU MEAN AND MEAN WHAT YOU SAY

JANET G CRUZ

For permissions requests, speaking inquiries, and bulk order purchase options, email: publishing@uconcept.com.

ISBN: 978-1-960188-18-2 | E-book

ISBN: 978-1-960188-19-9 | Paperback

ISBN: 978-1-960188-20-5 | Hardcover

Published by Unlimited Concepts, Coconut Creek, Florida.

www.publishing.uconcept.com

Book, Editing, and Cover Design by Janet M Garcia | UConceptDesigns.com

Published in the United States of America.

To the seekers of understanding,

In a world where voices clamor for attention, this book is dedicated to you. You, who understand that the art of communication extends far beyond the mere exchange of words. You, who recognize that true connection is forged in the quietude of listening, in the sacred space where hearts speak and souls listen.

To the unsung heroes in our lives – our parents, teachers, friends, and mentors – who, through their patient listening, have shaped our narratives and guided our steps. Your silent, yet profound influence is a testament to the profound impact of listening with intention.

CONTENTS

LEAVE A 1-CLICK REVIEW

Customer Reviews

⭐⭐⭐⭐⭐ 2
5.0 out of 5 stars ▼

5 star		100%
4 star		0%
3 star		0%
2 star		0%
1 star		0%

See all verified purchase reviews ›

Share your thoughts with other customers

Write a customer review

I would be incredibly thankful if you take just
60-seconds to write a brief review on Amazon,
even if it's just a few sentences!

https://shorturl.at/bilwN

INTRODUCTION

We humans love to talk! The entire history of humanity is a giant, sprawling conversation that spans continents, generations, and cultures. But here's the catch - we stink at it.

I know. It seems like a harsh thing to say. After all, we've been talking since pretty much the day we were born. But let's be honest with ourselves. How many times have we found ourselves misunderstood, or completely missing the point of what someone else was trying to say? Too many to count, right?

That's where this book comes in. Like you, I've had my fair share of communication breakdowns. Heck, I've even devoted my life learning about it while studying psychology and sociology. So, believe me when I say, I feel your pain, and I want to help.

You see, communication is more than just words. It's about understanding. Understanding what people mean, not just what they say. It's about reading between the lines, picking up on the unspoken signals we're constantly sending each other. It's about empathy, respect, and connection.

But perhaps most importantly, it's about *listening*. And I don't mean just hearing. I mean really listening - with your full attention, your heart open, and your ego checked at the door. Because when we truly listen, we not only understand others better, but we also understand ourselves.

That's why this book is more than just a guide to communicating effectively. It's a journey. A journey to bridge that communication gap we've all encountered. A journey to become a better listener, a better communicator, and ultimately, a better person.

So, get ready. We're about to take a deep dive into the heart and soul of human interaction. And trust me, it's a journey worth taking. Let's get started.

THE BUILDING BLOCKS OF
EFFECTIVE COMMUNICATION

*S*tep into a bustling coffee shop on a weekday morning, and you'll witness a symphony of communication. The barista shouting out orders, friends catching up over espresso, the business meeting unfold at a corner table. It's a grand confluence of words and gestures. Communication, in its truest form, is a dance between what's spoken and what's not, between the lines we utter and the cues we give and receive.

VERBAL AND NON-VERBAL: THE TWO SIDES OF COMMUNICATION

Think of it this way: communication is like a coin. It has two sides, each equally valuable. One side is verbal communication, the *words we say*. The other side? Non-verbal communication, the *cues we give* without uttering a word. Let's explore each side of the coin.

- **The Power of Words**

Words are our primary tool for expressing thoughts, ideas, and emotions. They're the building blocks that form sentences, paragraphs, and entire conversations. Do you remember the last time you found the perfect words to express how you felt? It's a powerful feeling, isn't it? The right words can bring clarity to chaos, comfort to distress, and understanding to confusion.

But here's the kicker: words, as potent as they are, make up only about 7% of our total communication. Shocking, right? But it's true. As much as we rely on words, they're just the tip of the iceberg when it comes to communication.

- **Non-Verbal Signals**

So, if words only make up 7%, what about the rest? The remaining 93% of our communication is non-verbal, encompassing things like body language, facial expressions, eye contact, and tone of voice.

Ever walked into a room and felt the tension without anyone saying a word? That's non-verbal communication at play. Or how about this: have you ever had someone say they're fine, but their crossed arms, clenched jaw, and diverted gaze screamed otherwise? Again, that's non-verbal communication.

Non-verbal cues can speak volumes. They can affirm or contradict what's being said verbally. They can reveal true feelings or intentions that words might not express. And they can set the tone and atmosphere of a conversation.

- **Balancing Verbal and Non-Verbal Cues**

So how do we balance these two sides of the communication coin? It's all about *alignment*.

Consider the experience of watching your favorite stand-up comedian. It's not just the jokes that get you laughing; it's also the way they deliver them. The timing, the facial expressions, the body language—all of these non-verbal cues amplify the humor in the words.

Similarly, in our everyday conversations, *alignment* between our words and non-verbal signals strengthens our message. If you're saying something serious, for example, leaning in slightly can show you're sincere. On the other hand, if you're sharing exciting news, your wide eyes and animated gestures can amplify your joy.

However, when our words say one thing and our body language says another, confusion ensues. For example, let's say you're at a networking event. You meet someone interesting, and you tell them, "I'd love to connect later and learn more about your work." But as you're saying this, you're glancing around the room, your body slightly turned away. The message sent? Despite your words, you're not truly interested.

Balancing verbal and non-verbal communication is a bit like tuning a guitar. If the strings (words) and the strumming (non-verbal cues) are in harmony, the music (communication) is beautiful. But if they're out of sync, it's just noise.

So, as we dive into the depths of effective communication, remember this: it's not just about finding the right words; it's also about aligning those words with our non-verbal cues to create clear, effective, and meaningful connections. It's about learning to dance gracefully through the symphony of communication. And trust me, with a little practice, we can all learn to dance.

DECODING THE UNSPOKEN: THE ROLE OF BODY LANGUAGE

Let's imagine you're at a party. You spot a friend across the room. Even from a distance, without hearing a single word, you can tell they're having a great time. Their broad smile, animated gestures, and the way they lean into the conversation—it's clear they're enjoying themselves. That, my friend, is the power of body language.

- **Reading Facial Expressions**

Our faces are like open books—they reveal what we feel. Happy, sad, surprised, disgusted, afraid—we have a unique facial expression for each emotion. Consider a time when you shared a joke with a friend. You didn't need them to say, "That's hilarious!" Their wide grin and the crinkle around their eyes said it all.

But, it's not just about identifying others' emotions. It's also about being aware of what our faces reveal. Ever tried to keep a poker face while bluffing during a card game? It's tough, right? That's because our faces often betray what we truly feel, even when our words might not.

- **Understanding Posture and Gestures**

Next up, let's talk about the rest of our body—our posture and gestures. Stand tall and straight, and you project confidence. Slump your shoulders and look down, you give off an air of insecurity.

Gestures, on the other hand, are like the punctuation marks in our spoken sentences. They add emphasis and clarity. A thumbs-up sign, a fist pump, a dismissive wave—each of these gestures can amplify or modify the meaning of our words.

Remember, though, that gestures can vary across cultures. A thumbs-up sign might be a mark of approval in one culture, but in another, it could be seen as rude. More on this when we dive into cultural communication nuances in a later chapter.

- **Interpreting Proximity and Personal Space**

Ever felt uncomfortable when someone stands too close to you? That's because they've invaded your personal space, the invisible bubble we all carry around us.

In general, the larger the bubble, the more formal or distant the relationship. Think about it. You're okay with your best friend sitting close to you on the couch, but you'd feel awkward if a mere acquaintance did the same.

Understanding this invisible boundary can help us gauge the level of comfort and intimacy in a relationship. It can also help us avoid making others uncomfortable by respecting their personal space.

- **Recognizing Eye Contact Patterns**

Lastly, let's talk about the eyes—the windows to the soul. Maintaining eye contact shows you're engaged and attentive. It signals respect and interest in the other person. However, just like Goldilocks and her porridge, the amount of eye contact needs to be just right. Too little, and you might come across as disinterested or dismissive. Too much, and you risk making the other person uncomfortable.

Eye contact patterns can also give us vital cues. For instance, if someone frequently looks away while talking, they might be nervous or unsure. On the other hand, if they maintain steady eye contact while listening, it signals that they're actively engaged in the conversation.

Alright, we've covered quite a bit of ground here. We've looked at how our faces, bodies, personal space, and eyes contribute to our communication. Each of these elements is like a piece of a puzzle that, when put together, gives us a complete picture of what's being communicated. So, as we move forward, let's keep this picture in mind. It'll be our guide as we navigate the intricate maze of human communication.

THE SOUND OF SILENCE: WHAT IT SAYS

Imagine that you're at a dinner party, and the host raises a glass for a toast. There's a moment of silence before they speak. That pause—it's electric. It draws you in, builds anticipation. That's the power of silence in communication. Far from being empty or void, *silence can be full of meaning*. It's an unspoken language all its own. And to truly excel at communication, we need to learn to understand and speak this language too.

- **Pauses and Their Meanings**

Let's start with pauses. They're the commas and full stops in our spoken sentences, giving rhythm to our speech. Without pauses, our words would rush past in a relentless, breathless stream, leaving listeners overwhelmed and confused.

But pauses are more than just breathing spaces. They can also carry meaning. A pause before answering a question, for example, can signal that you're thinking carefully about your response. A pause after a critical point can give listeners time to digest what's been said. A pause in the middle of a sentence can add suspense, drawing listeners in.

Here's an example. Imagine you're telling a friend about a thrilling movie you've watched. If you said, "And then, just when we thought the hero was done for, he...," and paused before revealing the climax, your friend would be hanging on your every word. That pause—it amplifies the suspense, making your story even more engaging.

Now, think about reading a book. The white spaces between words, sentences, and paragraphs give your eyes a brief rest, making the text easier to read and comprehend. In verbal communication, pauses serve a similar purpose. They give the listener time to process the information, enhancing their comprehension of your message.

When we pause, we allow our words to sink in, giving the listener a chance to absorb what we've said. It's like adding commas and full stops to our speech, making it more digestible and easier to understand.

• Silence as a Response

Now, let's look at silence as a response. In a conversation, if someone falls silent after you've said something, it can mean several things. It could be a sign of agreement, an indication that the person is taking in what you've said. It could be a sign of discomfort or disagreement, a non-confrontational way of saying, "I don't agree with you." Or it could simply mean the person is lost in thought, processing your words.

Let's say you're having a heated discussion with a colleague about a project. You lay out your points, and they fall silent. That silence —it's a moment of tension, isn't it? It's like a question hanging in the air: what are they thinking? Do they agree, disagree, or are they just processing what I've said?

Silence, in this context, is a cue for you to tune in, to observe their non-verbal signals, to gauge their reaction. And sometimes, it might also be a cue for you to step back, to give them space to think and respond.

• The Role of Silence in Active Listening

Finally, let's talk about silence in active listening. In our rush to respond or react, we often forget the value of silence. We fear that if we're silent, we'll be seen as disinterested, unresponsive, or—worst of all—awkward. But here's the truth: silence can be one of the most powerful tools in active listening.

When we are silent, we give the other person space to express themselves fully. We invite them to share more, to delve deeper.

We signal that we're not just waiting for our turn to speak—we're genuinely interested in understanding their perspective.

Imagine you're comforting a friend who's going through a tough time. They're sharing their feelings, their worries, their fears. As tempting as it might be to jump in with advice or reassurance, sometimes the best thing you can do is to stay silent. To listen, to empathize, to just be there for them. That silence—it's not empty. It's filled with understanding, compassion, and support.

So next time you find yourself in a conversation, remember this: silence is not your enemy. It's a friend, a tool, a language. Learn to use it, to understand it, to appreciate it. It's part of the dance of communication, a step that adds depth and meaning to your interactions. And as with any dance, it takes practice. But with time and patience, you'll find that you can dance with silence as effortlessly as you do with words.

THE IMPACT OF TONE: IT'S NOT JUST WHAT YOU SAY, BUT HOW YOU SAY IT

Imagine you're cheering on your favorite team at a sports match. The game is neck and neck, the tension is high, and you're on the edge of your seat. Suddenly, the commentator's voice comes on, monotone and devoid of any emotion. How does that feel? It takes the thrill out of the game, doesn't it? That's the impact of tone—it can make or break your communication.

- **Identifying Tone of Voice**

Tone of voice is like the background music in a movie scene—it sets the mood. It's not about the words you say, but how you say them. It's the difference between shouting "I love you!" in a romantic setting and whispering it during a heated argument. Same words, different tones, entirely different interpretations.

But how do you identify tone? Listen for changes in pitch, volume, and pace. A high pitch and fast pace often signal excitement or anxiety. A low pitch and slow pace can indicate calmness or boredom. Loudness can convey anger or enthusiasm, while softness might suggest intimacy or uncertainty.

- **The Influence of Tone on Message Reception**

The way we perceive a message is heavily influenced by the speaker's tone. Consider a simple phrase like, "Can you please close the door?" If said in a polite, friendly tone, it's an innocent request. But if spat out with a harsh, irritated tone, it sounds like an accusation. The words are identical in both scenarios, but the tone changes their meaning completely.

This is why it's crucial to pay attention to your tone, especially when discussing sensitive or emotional topics. Your words may be carefully chosen, but if your tone is off, it can lead to misunderstandings, hurt feelings, or conflict.

ADJUSTING TONE FOR EFFECTIVE COMMUNICATION

Learning to adjust your tone of voice is like learning to play a musical instrument. It takes practice, but once mastered, it opens up a whole new dimension of communication. Here are some tips to get you started.

- **Match the situation.** Your tone should suit the circumstances. A cheerful, upbeat tone is great for a party, but not so much for a funeral. A serious, focused tone works well in a business meeting, but it might kill the vibe at a casual get-together.

- **Reflect your emotions authentically.** If you're excited about something, let your tone reflect that excitement. If you're upset, don't be afraid to let your tone express that too. Authenticity builds trust and connection.

- **Consider the other person's feelings and needs.** If someone's had a rough day, a gentle, empathetic tone can be comforting. If they're excited about good news, match their enthusiasm with a lively, upbeat tone.

- **Be aware of cultural differences.** In some cultures, a loud, expressive tone is seen as friendly and engaging. In others, it might be perceived as aggressive or disrespectful. When communicating across cultures, it's essential to be aware of these nuances.

To illustrate these points, let's revisit that sports match. Picture the commentator now, their voice rising and falling with the action, their excitement matching yours. They shout when a goal is scored, their voice drops in suspense during penalties, and they talk fast during the most thrilling moments. That's the magic of tone—it draws you in, keeps you engaged, and makes the experience more vivid and memorable.

So, the next time you're in a conversation, remember to tune in to your tone. Listen to it, play with it, and adjust it as needed. It's a powerful tool in your communication toolkit, and when used effectively, it can transform your interactions.

And with that, we wrap up our exploration of the basic elements of effective communication. We've looked at the dance between words and silence, between what's spoken and what's unspoken. We've examined how our faces, bodies, eyes, and voices contribute to our communication. We've also seen how silence, far from being empty, can be filled with meaning.

As you step back into the hustle and bustle of your daily conversations, keep these insights in mind. Use them to tune into the subtle nuances of communication, to deepen your understanding of others, and to express yourself more clearly and effectively.

Remember, communication is not just about talking—it's about connecting. It's about seeing and being seen, understanding and being understood. And as we move forward, we'll delve deeper into this fascinating world, equipping you with the tools and strategies you need to become a truly effective communicator.

So, here's to communication—to the joy of understanding and being understood. May your conversations be clear, your connections deep, and your world a little brighter, one word, one gesture, one silence at a time.

BREAKING DOWN THE WALLS: THE PSYCHOLOGY OF COMMUNICATION

*P*icture this: you're at a crowded market, surrounded by a cacophony of sounds, colors, and movements. Now, imagine if every single stimulus demanded your equal attention. The aroma of the spices, the vibrant colors of the textiles, the loud haggling of the vendors, the jostling of the crowd - it would be overwhelming, right? Luckily, our brains are designed to filter and prioritize information, helping us navigate this sensory overload with ease. This information processing is the foundation of how we communicate, and understanding it can unlock new pathways to effective communication.

THE HUMAN BRAIN: HOW WE PROCESS INFORMATION

And so, we find ourselves at the doorstep of the most complex structure in the universe - the human brain. It's a marvel of nature, capable of processing vast amounts of information in the blink of an eye. But how exactly does it do this? Let's take a peek inside.

- **The Role of the Left and Right Brain Hemispheres**

The first thing to note is that our brain is divided into two hemispheres - the left and the right. Picture yourself holding a map. The left hemisphere is your navigator, dealing with logic, analysis, and details. It's the side that breaks down the map into streets, landmarks, and directions. The right hemisphere, on the other hand, is your explorer. It's all about imagination, intuition, and the big picture. It's the side that appreciates the beauty of the landscape, the thrill of the journey.

These two sides work in tandem when we communicate. The left brain processes the words and grammar of a sentence, while the right brain interprets the tone, context, and emotional content. In a sense, *the left brain hears the notes, while the right brain listens to the music.*

- **The Impact of Emotions on Processing Information**

Ever noticed how some memories, especially emotional ones, are so vivid? That's because emotions play a crucial role in how we process and remember information.

Think about the last time you watched a thrilling movie. The racing heartbeat during the chase scenes, the lump in your throat during the emotional climax - these intense emotions etch the experience into your memory.

The same principle applies to communication. When a conversation stirs strong emotions, the information hits harder and sticks longer. That's why emotional stories often make the most impact. They bypass the brain's logic filters and strike directly at the heart.

- **The Influence of Past Experiences on Perception**

Our past experiences, too, play a significant role in shaping our communication. Imagine you're learning to play a musical instrument. At first, every note, every chord seems alien. But with practice, your brain starts recognizing patterns. Soon, you're not just playing notes - you're making music.

Similarly, our past experiences in communication shape our present perceptions. They form a mental database of words, expressions, and tones that we draw upon in every conversation. A raised voice might signal anger to someone who grew up in a loud household, while someone else might see it as a sign of excitement.

However, this database isn't set in stone. It can be updated, refined, and expanded with new experiences. Ever learned a new word and then suddenly started noticing it everywhere? That's your mental database in action, updating itself in real-time.

So, there you have it - a sneak peek into the human brain and how it processes information. It's a fascinating interplay of logic and imagination, emotion and experience, all working together to make sense of the world around us. And as we continue our exploration of communication, we'll see how these elements come into play, shaping not just how we talk, but how we listen, understand, and connect with others.

But for now, let's marvel at the beauty and complexity of our brains. They're not just organs, but intricate symphonies of neurons, humming with the music of thoughts, emotions, and memories. And it's this symphony that forms the backdrop of our communication, setting the stage for the dance of words, silence, and understanding.

So, as you go about your day, remember this: every word you speak, every word you hear, is a testament to the marvel that is your brain. It's the silent conductor of your communication symphony, orchestrating a masterpiece of understanding and connection. And as we delve deeper into the psychology of communication, we'll learn to appreciate this symphony, to listen to its music, and to play our part in it with grace, empathy, and understanding.

EMOTIONAL INTELLIGENCE: THE KEY TO EMPATHETIC COMMUNICATION

When it comes to communication, there's a secret ingredient that can elevate it from good to great. No, it's not a fancy vocabulary or eloquent speech. It's something much more fundamental - *emotional intelligence.*

Emotional intelligence, or EI, is the ability to identify, understand, and manage our own emotions and the emotions of others. It's like having an internal compass that helps us navigate the complex landscape of feelings that color our communication. Let's delve into this fascinating concept, piece by piece.

- **Understanding Your Emotions**

Think back to the last time you felt upset. Maybe your boss criticized your work, or a friend canceled plans at the last minute. Now, how did you react? Did you lash out in anger, or did you take a moment to understand why you felt upset?

See, *understanding our emotions* is the first step towards emotional intelligence. It's about looking inwards, acknowledging what we're feeling, and understanding why we're feeling that way. It's like being a detective of our own minds, piecing together the clues of our emotional reactions.

But how exactly do we do this? It starts by tuning into our bodies. Often, our bodies signal our emotions before we can put them into words. A knot in the stomach, a racing heart, a furrowed brow - these are all physical manifestations of our emotions. By paying attention to these signals, we can start to understand our emotions better.

Next, we need to reflect on our emotions. This can be as simple as taking a few quiet moments to check in with ourselves throughout the day. Or it could involve journaling, meditation, or other mindfulness practices. The goal is to create a space where we can observe our emotions without judgment, allowing us to understand them better.

- **Recognizing Others' Emotions**

Now, let's turn our gaze outwards. Emotional intelligence isn't just about understanding our own emotions - it's also about tuning into the feelings of others.

Remember the last time you shared a problem with a friend? Did they offer advice, or did they simply listen and validate your feelings? If they did the latter, you've experienced the power of emotional recognition. It's the ability to sense and acknowledge what someone else is feeling, creating a connection that goes beyond words.

But how do we cultivate this ability? Again, it starts with *observation*. Pay close attention to the other person's words, tone of voice, body language, and facial expressions. These are all clues to their emotional state.

Next, *practice empathy*. Try to put yourself in the other person's shoes. How might they be feeling? What might they be thinking? Empathy is like a bridge that connects you to the emotional world of others, enriching your communication with understanding and compassion.

- **Managing Emotional Responses**

Lastly, emotional intelligence involves managing our emotional responses, both in ourselves and in our interactions with others.

Let's say you're in a heated discussion with a colleague. You feel your anger rising, your heart pounding, your fists clenching. In that moment, managing your emotional response could mean taking a few deep breaths, stepping away for a moment, or using calming self-talk.

Similarly, when dealing with others, managing emotional responses could involve using calming language, offering reassurance, or simply providing a safe space for the other person to express their feelings.

But remember, managing emotions doesn't mean suppressing them. It's not about putting on a happy face and pretending everything's fine when it's not. It's about acknowledging our feelings, understanding them, and then choosing a response that aligns with our values and the situation at hand.

So, there you have it - emotional intelligence, the secret sauce of effective communication. It's about tuning into our own emotions, recognizing the emotions of others, and managing our emotional responses. It's a skill that can transform our communication, fostering deeper connections, greater understanding, and more fulfilling interactions.

As you continue your exploration of communication, keep these insights in mind. Practice observing your emotions, empathizing with others, and managing your emotional responses. Over time, you'll find that these practices become second nature, enriching your communication with the depth and richness of emotional intelligence.

So, let's celebrate emotional intelligence - the silent symphony that plays in every conversation, the invisible thread that connects us all. It's a testament to our shared humanity, a reminder of our capacity for empathy and understanding. And as we tune into this symphony, as we strengthen this thread, we step closer to the heart of effective communication - the joy of true connection.

THE POWER OF PERCEPTION: HOW IT INFLUENCES UNDERSTANDING

- **Confirmation Bias**

Confirmation bias is the tendency to focus on information that confirms our pre-existing beliefs and ignore the information that contradicts them. Kind of like when you're trying to solve a puzzle, and you're convinced that a particular piece fits in a specific spot. You keep trying, ignoring the other pieces that could potentially fit.

In active listening, confirmation bias *can lead us to hear only what we want to hear.* We become selective listeners, cherry-picking the parts of the conversation that align with our views and disregarding the parts that don't. This can result in misunderstandings and misinterpretations, hindering effective communication.

To overcome this bias, we need to approach conversations with an open mind, ready to consider different perspectives. It's about being aware of our preconceived notions and being willing to challenge them. It's like approaching the puzzle with flexibility, open to the possibility that the piece could fit somewhere else.

- **Perception and Reality**

Close your eyes. Now, picture an apple. Easy, right? You can see the shiny skin, the vibrant red color, perhaps even feel the crisp crunch as you bite into it. Now, open your eyes and look around. How do we know that the apple you're picturing and the real apple you're seeing are the same? It's all down to perception.

Perception is the brain's way of interpreting what our senses tell us, transforming sensory input into our own personal picture of reality. It's like a mental paintbrush, coloring our world with the hues of our past experiences, emotions, and biases.

Think about the last time you met someone new. Within seconds, you formed a first impression, right? You sized them up, made a few quick judgments. That's your perception paintbrush at work, filling in the details based on your past experiences and preconceptions.

But here's the catch. Our perception paintbrush isn't always accurate. It's influenced by our biases, our blind spots, and our emotional state at the moment. That's why two people can have very different perceptions of the same event. It's not that one person is right and the other is wrong; it's just that their paintbrushes are using different colors.

BIASES AND PREJUDICES: HOW THEY IMPACT LISTENING

Imagine you're exploring a forest. Your path is clear, the sunlight is peeking through the trees, and you're enjoying the sounds of nature. Suddenly, you spot a snake slithering across your path. You freeze, your heart pounds, and your peaceful exploration turns into a stressful encounter. That's what biases and prejudices can do to our listening. They're like snakes on our path, introducing stress and fear, and disrupting our peaceful exploration of the conversation. Let's delve into some common biases and prejudices and see how they can impact our listening.

- **The Influence of Bias on Perception**

We all have biases. They're mental shortcuts, helping us make sense of the world around us. But these biases can also cloud our perception, skewing our understanding of reality.

Take confirmation bias, for instance. This is the tendency to favor information that confirms our pre-existing beliefs and ignore information that contradicts them. Imagine you're convinced that your favorite soccer team is the best. You'll remember every win, every spectacular goal they score. But you might conveniently forget the games they lost or the goals they missed. Or consider the halo effect.

- **Halo Effect**

The halo effect is when our overall impression of someone influences how we perceive their individual traits. If you like someone, you're likely to perceive everything they do in a positive light. If you dislike them, you're likely to interpret their actions negatively.

Maybe they have a warm smile, an engaging personality, or a common interest with you. This instant liking can color your perception of everything else about them.

In active listening, the halo effect can lead us to overestimate the speaker's credibility or likability. It's like putting on rose-colored glasses, where everything looks rosy and pleasant. This can distort our understanding, leading us to overlook important details or cues.

To counter the halo effect, we need to strive for a balanced perspective, recognizing that everyone has a mix of strengths and weaknesses. It's about taking off the rose-colored glasses and seeing the person in their true light.

These biases, and many others, can distort our perception, leading to misunderstandings and miscommunication. They can make us jump to conclusions, judge too quickly, or misinterpret what others are saying.

- **Strategies for Clearing Perception Filters**

So, how do we clear these perception filters? How do we make sure our perception paintbrush is painting an accurate picture of reality? Let's explore a few strategies.

First, we need to become aware of our biases. It's like cleaning our glasses - we first need to know they're dirty. This might involve reflecting on our past interactions, noticing patterns in our judgments, or seeking feedback from others.

Next, we can practice mindfulness. This is about being present in the moment, observing without judging. It's like watching a movie without critiquing the plot or the acting, just taking in the scenes as they unfold. When we practice mindfulness in our communication, we listen more fully, perceive more accurately, and understand more deeply.

Finally, we can *cultivate empathy*. This is about stepping into the other person's shoes, seeing the world through their eyes. When we do this, we move beyond our own perception filters, opening up to a broader, more inclusive understanding.

And there you have it - a closer look at the role of perception in communication. It's a fascinating aspect, adding depth and complexity to our interactions. And by becoming aware of our perception filters and learning to clear them, we can enhance our understanding, foster deeper connections, and communicate more effectively.

So, as you navigate your everyday conversations, remember to check in with your perception. Notice the color of your paintbrush, the size of your canvas, the filters on your lenses. And with each conversation, each interaction, strive to perceive more clearly, understand more deeply, and communicate more effectively. It's not always easy, but it's always worth it. After all, clear perception is more than just seeing - it's truly understanding. And in the dance of communication, understanding is the rhythm that keeps us in step, the music that moves us, the connection that brings us closer.

PERSONALITY TYPES AND COMMUNICATION STYLES: HOW THEY INTERACT

Have you ever met someone and felt an instant click? Your conversations flow seamlessly, as if you're singing from the same song sheet. On the flip side, you might have encountered individuals where communication feels like trying to fit a square peg into a round hole. There's a reason for this harmony or discord, and it lies in the realm of *personality types* and *communication styles*.

- **Identifying Your Personality Type**

Imagine you're at a party. Do you gravitate towards the center of the room, basking in the energy of the crowd, or do you find solace in a quiet corner, engaging in one-on-one conversations? Your preference could offer a clue about your personality type.

Various models categorize personality types, but let's focus on the Myers-Briggs Type Indicator (MBTI) for its widespread recognition and use. This model classifies individuals into 16 personality types based on four dichotomies: Extraversion vs. Introversion, Sensing vs. Intuition, Thinking vs. Feeling, and Judging vs. Perceiving.

Your personality type significantly influences your communication style. For instance, if you lean towards extraversion, you might be more outspoken and thrive on active, dynamic conversations. On the other hand, if you're more introverted, you might prefer listening and partake in thoughtful, contemplative dialogue.

Identifying your personality type is like getting a map of your communication landscape. It sheds light on your natural inclinations, your strengths, and areas where you might need to stretch and grow.

- **Understanding Others' Personality Types**

So, you've started to understand your personality type. Now, let's flip the coin. Just as your personality influences your communication style, the same applies to the people around you.

The challenge here is that we can't peek into someone's brain to understand their personality type. We have to rely on observation and interaction. You might notice a colleague who meticulously plans their tasks and prefers structured meetings (indicative of a Judging type). Or a friend who easily adapts to sudden changes in plans and thrives in spontaneous conversations (a hint towards the Perceiving type).

Recognizing others' personality types can help you tailor your communication accordingly. It's like learning to speak someone else's language. It might feel awkward and challenging at first, but with practice, it can lead to more harmonious and effective communication.

- **Adapting Communication to Different Personality Styles**

Now comes the real test - adapting your communication style based on different personality types. It's as much an art as it is a science, a delicate dance of adjusting and aligning your communication rhythm to match your partner's.

For instance, if you're an extroverted individual interacting with an introverted colleague, you might need to dial down your energy a bit, giving them space to express their thoughts. Or, if you're a person who leans towards the Feeling preference, you might need to focus more on logic and facts when communicating with a Thinking type.

Remember, adapting doesn't mean changing who you are. It's about flexing your communication muscles, stretching a little out of your comfort zone for the sake of better connection and understanding. It's about showing respect for the other person's communication style and making an effort to meet them halfway.

So, there you have it - an exploration of how personality types interact with communication styles. It's a fascinating realm, offering insights that can transform the way you communicate and connect with others.

As you continue your day, keep these insights in mind. Try identifying your personality type and observe those of the people around you. Notice how these personality types influence communication styles. And most importantly, practice adapting your communication to different personality styles.

It might feel like a challenge at first, like trying to dance to a song you've never heard before. But with practice, patience, and persistence, you'll find your rhythm. You'll start to appreciate the unique melody of each personality type, the distinct rhythm of each communication style. And in doing so, you'll unlock a whole new level of connection and understanding - a harmony that resonates beyond words, touching the very heart of human connection.

As we move forward, we'll continue to build on these insights, equipping you with more tools and strategies to enhance your communication. So, stay tuned, stay curious, and keep practicing. The dance floor of communication awaits, and with each step, you're becoming a more skillful, more empathetic, and more effective dancer.

ACTIVE LISTENING: THE UNSUNG HERO OF EFFECTIVE COMMUNICATION

*I*magine you're tuning into your favorite radio station. The music flows, filling the room with rhythm and melody. But suddenly, there's a crackle, and the music is replaced by static. Frustrating, isn't it? Communication can be similar. When we focus more on speaking than listening, it's like turning up the static and drowning out the music. The result? Misunderstandings, missed opportunities, and a breakdown in connection. But there's a solution to turn down the static and tune back into the music: *Active Listening.*

Active Listening is more than just hearing the words being said. It's full engagement in the conversation, a two-way street where you're not just taking in words, but also understanding the underlying emotions, intentions, and messages. It's the art of being present, of showing the speaker that you value what they're saying. And it's not just about making the speaker feel heard, but also about enhancing your understanding, empathy, and connection.

THE TECHNIQUES OF ACTIVE LISTENING

Active Listening involves a set of techniques that help us tune in more effectively to the speaker. These techniques are straightforward, but like any skill, they require practice to master. Let's explore each of them.

- **Reflective Statements**

Think of the last time you shared a problem with a friend. If they responded with, "It sounds like you're really upset about this," they used a reflective statement. Reflective statements are like mirrors, echoing back the speaker's feelings or statements. They show that you're not just hearing the words, but also understanding the emotions and intentions behind them.

- **Paraphrasing**

Remember when you had to write a book report in school? You had to take the story and retell it in your own words. That's paraphrasing. In Active Listening, paraphrasing serves a similar purpose. It's about rephrasing the speaker's words in your own way. This not only shows that you're actively engaged, but also gives the speaker a chance to clarify if you've misinterpreted something.

- **Summarizing**

Summarizing is like creating a highlight reel of the conversation. It involves pulling together the main points and presenting them back to the speaker. This can be especially helpful in longer conversations, where key points could get lost in the flow. A good summary reaffirms your understanding and gives the speaker a chance to add or correct anything that's been missed.

- **Clarifying Questions**

Ever been lost while following a map, and you had to ask a passerby for directions? Clarifying questions in Active Listening serve a similar purpose. They're your way of asking for directions when the conversation becomes unclear. They could be as simple as, "Could you explain what you meant by..." or "When you said..., did you mean...?"

- **Non-Verbal Signals**

Non-verbal signals are like the background music in a movie scene. They set the mood and amplify the message. In Active Listening, non-verbal signals involve showing engagement through your body language. This could be maintaining eye contact, nodding in agreement, or leaning in slightly towards the speaker.

Each of these techniques adds a unique note to the symphony of Active Listening. They show the speaker that you're not just hearing the words, but also tuning into the music behind them. And when used together, they create a harmony that enhances understanding, fosters connection, and turns down the static in communication.

So, the next time you find yourself in a conversation, remember these techniques. Practice them, play with them, and make them your own. Active Listening might not always be easy, but it's always worth it. After all, when we truly listen, we not only understand others better, but we also understand ourselves. And that's a tune worth dancing to.

THE FEEDBACK LOOP: ENSURING THE MESSAGE IS UNDERSTOOD

Imagine you're playing a game of catch. You throw the ball, your friend catches it, and throws it back. Simple, right? Now, think of communication as a game of catch. You throw ideas, feelings, or thoughts, and the receiver catches them. But how do you know if they've genuinely caught what you intended? Here's where the feedback loop comes in. It's the process of confirming that your message has been received and understood accurately. Let's break it down into three actionable steps.

- **Verbal Confirmation**

First off, let's discuss verbal confirmation. You know, those little nods of understanding we give during a conversation like "Mhmm," "Right," "I see," and so forth. They might seem insignificant, but they play a crucial role in the communication process. These simple affirmations act as signposts, signaling to the speaker that you're following along, catching the ideas they're throwing your way.

But here's the thing about verbal confirmation—it's a two-way street. When you're the one doing the talking, encourage the listener to give these verbal nods. You could do this by pausing occasionally, making eye contact, or simply asking, "Are you with me so far?" This way, you're not just throwing balls blindly. You're making sure they're being caught.

- **Paraphrase and Ask for Confirmation**

Next up is paraphrasing. Think of it like catching the ball, examining it, and then describing it to the thrower. By paraphrasing what the speaker said, you're showing that you've not only caught their message but also understood it.

Here's an example. If a friend tells you, "I'm worried that I might lose my job because of the budget cuts," you could paraphrase it as, "So, you're feeling anxious about the possibility of job loss due to the company's financial issues." Notice how this isn't just a repetition of what they said. It's a restatement, reflecting your understanding of their message.

Once you've paraphrased, don't stop there. Ask for confirmation. A simple, "Did I get that right?" or "Is that what you meant?" can make a world of difference. It gives the speaker a chance to clarify, correct, or confirm, ensuring that you're both on the same page.

- **Use Open-Ended Questions**

Finally, let's talk about open-ended questions. They're like throwing the ball back with a spin, encouraging the speaker to add more detail or depth to their message.

Open-ended questions are broad, inviting the speaker to elaborate, explain, or expand on their point. They're not just a "yes" or "no" kind of deal. They require more thought, more introspection. Questions like, "How did that make you feel?" or "What do you think is the best way forward?" fall into this category.

By asking open-ended questions, you're not just confirming that you've understood the message. You're also showing genuine interest, encouraging the speaker to share more. It's a powerful way to deepen the conversation, fostering greater understanding and connection.

And there you have it—the feedback loop in all its glory. It's a simple yet effective process, ensuring that your game of communication catch is successful. By using verbal confirmation, paraphrasing, and open-ended questions, you're not just catching the messages thrown your way. You're also making sure you've caught them right, understood them deeply, and are ready to throw back meaningfully.

So, the next time you find yourself in a conversation, remember these steps. Practice verbal confirmation, get comfortable with paraphrasing, and don't shy away from asking open-ended questions. They might seem small, but their impact is immense. They transform your listening from passive to active, from surface-level to deep, from static-filled to clear as a bell.

And in the end, isn't that what true communication is all about? It's not just about talking or hearing. It's about understanding and being understood. It's about connecting, not just on the surface, but deep down where it really counts. So, here's to active listening, to the feedback loop, to the game of communication catch. May your throws be clear, your catches be sure, and your game be a joy to play.

- **The Challenges of Active Listening**

Active Listening is like navigating a maze. It's about finding your way through a labyrinth of words, tones, and emotions, seeking understanding, connection, and empathy at the end. But just like any maze, there can be obstacles along the way. Let's explore some of these challenges and how they can hinder our journey to becoming effective active listeners.

- **Emotional Triggers**

Think about this: you're having a calm, amicable conversation with a friend. Suddenly, they mention something - a person, a topic, a phrase - that hits a raw nerve. Your heart rate spikes, your palms sweat, and your mind races. That, my friend, is an emotional trigger.

Emotional triggers are *personal hot buttons* that evoke strong emotional reactions. They're like invisible tripwires, hiding in the corners of our mind, ready to catch us off guard. When triggered, our emotional reactions can hijack our ability to listen actively. We might become defensive, withdrawn, or reactive, hindering our ability to understand and empathize with the speaker.

- **Preconceived Notions**

We all have them - beliefs, opinions, assumptions we hold about people, situations, or topics. They're like tinted glasses, coloring the way we see the world. In active listening, these preconceived notions can distort our understanding.

For instance, if you hold a certain stereotype about a group of people, it might influence how you interpret what a member of that group says. Or if you've had a disagreement with someone in the past, it might affect your willingness to listen to them openly in the future. In both cases, your preconceived notions act as filters, potentially skewing your perception and understanding.

- **Distractions**

Picture yourself in a bustling cafe, trying to have a heart-to-heart with a friend. The clatter of dishes, the chatter of customers, the whirl of the espresso machine - they're all competing for your attention. These distractions can make active listening a challenge.

Distractions aren't just external; they can be internal too. Worries about an upcoming deadline, excitement about a weekend trip, or simply daydreaming can pull your focus away from the conversation. In both cases, distractions can make it hard to stay present and engaged in the conversation, hindering your ability to listen actively.

- **Lack of Interest in the Topic**

Let's face it - not every conversation topic is going to light a spark of interest. Maybe your colleague is passionate about bird watching, but you can't tell a sparrow from a seagull. Or perhaps your friend loves discussing politics, while you prefer talking about sports or movies.

When the topic doesn't interest you, active listening can become a struggle. You might find your attention wandering, your mind zoning out. And when you're not fully engaged, your ability to understand and connect with the speaker diminishes.

- **Personal Bias**

Personal bias is like a spotlight in a dark room. It highlights what aligns with our beliefs and shadows what doesn't. In active listening, personal bias can lead us to hear what we want to hear, ignoring or dismissing what doesn't fit our views.

For example, if you believe that your boss is always critical, you might focus only on their negative feedback, overlooking any praise or positive comments. This bias can lead to selective listening, skewing your understanding and potentially straining your relationship.

So, there you have it - the challenges of active listening. They're like bumps on the road, hurdles on the track, thorns on the rose stem. They can make our journey to effective active listening a bit tricky. But here's the good news: awareness is the first step towards overcoming these challenges. By recognizing these hurdles, we're better equipped to tackle them, clearing the path towards understanding, empathy, and connection.

So, as you navigate your conversations, keep these challenges in mind. Notice when you encounter them, acknowledge their presence, and remember - they're not roadblocks, just speed bumps. With patience, practice, and a bit of perseverance, you can navigate around them, keeping your journey to effective active listening on track.

And remember, active listening isn't about being a perfect listener. It's about striving to understand, to connect, to truly hear the music behind the words. It's about turning down the static and tuning into the symphony of understanding. And with each conversation, each interaction, you're tuning in a little bit more, dancing a little bit closer to the heart of communication.

THE BENEFITS OF ACTIVE LISTENING: BETTER RELATIONSHIPS, FEWER MISUNDERSTANDINGS

Imagine now that you're climbing a mountain. The air is thin, the climb is steep, but the view at the peak is worth it. Active Listening is a lot like that climb. It can be challenging, but the rewards are truly worth the effort. Let's take a look at some of these benefits.

- **Enhanced Relationship Building**

Consider a favorite restaurant. What makes it special? Is it just the food, or is it the welcoming atmosphere, the attentive service, the feeling of being valued? Active Listening creates a similar environment in our interactions.

When we actively listen, we signal to the other person that we value their thoughts and feelings. We create a space where they feel safe to express themselves freely. This can strengthen existing relationships and foster new ones. It's like laying a strong foundation for a house, providing stability and strength for the structure built on top.

- **Improved Trust and Cooperation**

Picture a team game. Trust and cooperation are the lifeblood of a well-functioning team. Without them, the team crumbles. Active Listening fosters these essential elements in our interactions.

By showing that we truly understand what the other person is saying, we build trust. And where there's trust, there's a willingness to cooperate, to work together towards a common goal. It's like the glue that binds a team, making it stronger and more effective.

- **Conflict Prevention**

Imagine a garden. Left untended, weeds can overrun it, choking the life out of the plants. Misunderstandings in communication are like those weeds. If left unaddressed, they can lead to conflicts, damaging relationships. Active Listening is like a diligent gardener, nipping misunderstandings in the bud before they turn into conflicts.

By ensuring that we understand what the other person is saying, we can address any misconceptions right away. This can prevent minor misunderstandings from escalating into major conflicts, preserving the harmony of our interactions.

- **Increased Understanding and Empathy**

Think of a book now. The more you read, the more you understand the characters, their motivations, their emotions. Active Listening allows us to read the book of human interaction with more depth and understanding.

By truly tuning into what the other person is saying, we not only understand their words but also their emotions, perspectives, and experiences. This can increase our empathy, allowing us to connect with them on a deeper level. It's like stepping into their shoes, seeing the world through their eyes.

So, there you have it: the fruits of the Active Listening climb. Each one is a testament to the power of truly listening to understand, not just to respond. Each one is a reward for the effort we put into navigating the labyrinth of human interaction.

As we continue to develop our Active Listening skills, we'll find these benefits seeping into all areas of our lives. Our relationships will deepen, our conflicts will lessen, and our understanding of others and ourselves will grow. And in the end, isn't that the true goal of communication? It's more than just words and sentences; it's about connection, understanding, and empathy. Remember, it's about turning down the static and tuning into the symphony of human interaction.

Always keep in mind that Active Listening isn't just a skill; *it's a mindset.* It's about being present, being attentive, being empathetic. It's about truly hearing the music behind the words, the emotions behind the ideas, the humans behind the voices. And as you continue to practice, you'll find the climb becoming easier, the view becoming clearer, and the music becoming sweeter.

And on that note, let's prepare to explore further into the wonderful realm of effective communication. There's much more to discover, many more peaks to conquer. So, hold tight, stay curious, and keep climbing. The view at the top is worth it.

OVERCOMING BARRIERS TO EFFECTIVE LISTENING

*H*ave you ever tried to tune into a faint radio station while you're driving through a tunnel? The signal is weak, the static is strong, and you strain your ears to catch the melody amidst the noise. This is a lot like trying to listen effectively in a world swarming with distractions. It's an uphill battle, trying to focus on the message when the noise around us and within us is constantly competing for our attention. But fear not! Just like finding that sweet spot on the radio dial where the signal comes in clear, there are ways to tune into the conversation and turn down the distractions. Let's explore the first of these barriers.

THE NOISE AROUND US: PHYSICAL AND MENTAL DISTRACTIONS

- **Environmental Noise**

Imagine now trying to have a deep conversation at a busy airport terminal. The constant announcements, the crowds bustling by, the squeaky wheels of luggage trolleys - it's like trying to listen to a whisper at a rock concert. This environmental noise can make active listening a challenge. It's not just about the volume, but also the unpredictability. The sudden honk of a car, the shrill ring of a phone, the persistent drip of a leaky faucet - these unexpected sounds can easily jolt us out of our focus.

So, what can we do? Where possible, choose a quiet, comfortable setting for important conversations. If that's not an option, use tools to control the noise - earplugs, noise-canceling headphones, or even a white noise app. And sometimes, the best solution might be to simply acknowledge the noise and agree to continue the conversation at a later time or a different place.

- **Digital Distractions**

Then come the digital distractions. The ping of a new email, the buzz of a text message, the lure of social media notifications - they're like shiny baubles, constantly tugging at our attention. In the blink of an eye, we can find ourselves scrolling through our feeds, completely oblivious to the conversation at hand.

The solution? The silent mode on our devices is a godsend. Use it liberally during conversations. Better yet, keep your device out of sight to resist the temptation of a sneak peek. And remember, it's not just about curbing your own digital distractions, but also respecting the other person's time and attention by not interrupting the conversation with unnecessary digital detours.

I remember one time I went out to dinner with a friend. The minute we sat at the table, she started going through her social media on the phone. I stayed quiet for a while. More than ten minutes passed. No conversation. Then I looked around and noticed that no one around was not talking either. They were all glued to their phones too. No conversation, no bonding... I thought to myself: What's the point of going out for dinner with my friend if she is going to be glued to her phone. I'd rather stay home doing something productive! You get the point!

- **Internal Distractions**

Not all distractions come from the outside. Sometimes, the noise inside our heads can be just as disruptive. Worries about an upcoming presentation, planning a grocery list, replaying an argument - our minds can be a whirlwind of thoughts, pulling us away from the conversation.

One way to quieten this internal chatter is by practicing *mindfulness*. It's about anchoring yourself in the present moment, gently bringing your attention back to the conversation whenever it wanders. It's not about emptying your mind, but about *acknowledging your thoughts* without getting swept away by them.

- **Emotional Distractions**

Last, but certainly not least, are emotional distractions. If you're feeling upset, anxious, or excited, it can color your perception of the conversation. It's like looking through tinted glasses - the color of your emotions can distort the true colors of the message.

Managing emotional distractions involves recognizing and acknowledging your emotions. It's okay to tell the other person, "I'm feeling a bit upset right now, and it's making it hard for me to focus. Can we continue this conversation later?" By addressing your emotions, you're not only taking care of your mental well-being but also making sure that your emotional state doesn't hinder your ability to listen actively.

So, there you have it - the noise that surrounds us and how to turn it down. Each of these distractions is like a hurdle on the track to effective listening. But with awareness and a few handy strategies, we can overcome these hurdles. We can tune into the conversation, turn down the distractions, and enjoy the symphony of understanding that comes with effective listening.

Remember, listening isn't just about the ears - it's also about the mind. It's about clearing the static, quieting the noise, and tuning into the melody of the message. It's about being present, being focused, being truly engaged in the conversation. So, as you navigate your conversations, keep these distractions in mind. Notice them, manage them, and don't let them tune you out of the music of understanding. Because in the end, that's what effective listening is all about - it's about turning down the static and tuning into the symphony. It's about hearing the words, understanding the message, and dancing to the music of connection. And with each conversation, each interaction, you're tuning in a little bit more, dancing a little bit closer to the heart of communication.

- **Stereotyping**

Stereotyping involves making assumptions about the speaker based on their group membership, such as their race, religion, gender, or age. It's similar to when everyone is wearing a mask, and you're trying to guess who's behind each one based on limited information.

Stereotyping can cloud our listening, leading us to make premature judgments about the speaker. It's like trying to understand the person behind the mask based on the mask alone. This can limit our understanding and empathy, reducing the depth and richness of our conversations.

To avoid stereotyping, we need to remind ourselves that every individual is unique, with their own thoughts, feelings, and experiences. We need to listen to the person, not the group they belong to. It's about looking beyond the mask, eager to discover the unique individual behind it.

- **Selective Perception**

Selective perception involves focusing on the aspects of the conversation that resonate with our interests, beliefs, or needs, and tuning out the rest. Think of it like tuning into a radio station. You adjust the dial until you find the station that plays your favorite music, tuning out the rest.

Selective perception can limit our understanding of the full message, leading us to miss out on important details or perspectives. It's like listening to the same radio station all the time, missing out on the variety and richness of other stations.

To tackle selective perception, we need to broaden our listening, tuning into the full spectrum of the conversation. It's like exploring different radio stations, appreciating the diverse music they offer.

So, there you have it. By recognizing and prejudices, and learning to navigate around them, we can ensure a smoother journey. We can tune into the conversation more fully, turning down the static of biases, and tuning into the symphony of understanding. This is what active listening is all about.

Let's continue our exploration of effective listening, diving deeper into the challenges and strategies that can enhance our listening skills. We'll look at the pitfalls of multitasking, the role of patience and focus, and much more. So, stay tuned, stay curious, and keep dancing.

THE PROBLEM OF MULTITASKING

Imagine you're at a circus, watching a juggler. He's got three balls in the air, his eyes darting from one to another, his hands moving in a rapid, rhythmic dance. It's impressive, isn't it? Now, imagine yourself as that juggler, but the balls you're juggling are not made of rubber—they're your tasks, your responsibilities, your conversations. Welcome to the world of multitasking.

Multitasking, at first glance, might seem like a smart move. After all, why tackle one task when you can handle two or three at the same time? But here's the catch—when it comes to listening, multitasking can be a stumbling block. It's like trying to watch a movie, read a book, and follow a recipe all at once. Sooner or later, something's going to get burnt, missed, or misunderstood. Let's explore how multitasking can impact our ability to listen effectively. In active listening, multitasking can be a major roadblock.

It dilutes our focus, reduces our comprehension, and hampers our ability to connect with the speaker.

- **Decreased Concentration**

Let's start with the impact on our concentration. When we multitask, our attention is divided between the conversation and the other tasks at hand. It's like trying to watch a movie while cooking dinner - you'll likely miss important scenes or burn the food. Similarly, multitasking during a conversation can lead to missed details, misunderstood information, or superficial understanding.

- **Increased Errors**

Next, let's consider the risk of errors. When juggling multiple tasks, it's easy to drop a ball. In a conversation, this could mean mishearing a word, misunderstanding a point, or misinterpreting a message. These errors can lead to miscommunication, confusion, or even conflict.

- **Lowered Productivity**

Multitasking also affects our productivity. It might seem like we're getting more done by doing multiple things at once. But in reality, it often takes longer to complete tasks when we're switching back and forth between them. This is because each switch requires our brain to refocus, which takes time and energy.

- **Reduced Retention**

Lastly, multitasking can affect our retention of information. When our attention is divided, it's harder for our brain to encode and store information. This can lead to forgetfulness or a vague recollection of the conversation.

So, how do we overcome the challenge of multitasking? It all boils down to one thing – *focus (single-tasking)*. By giving the conversation our undivided attention, we can enhance our understanding, reduce errors, improve productivity, and boost retention. It's like watching a movie without distractions - you're more likely to appreciate the plot, remember the details, and enjoy the experience. It's about appreciating the richness of the dialogue, the nuances of the speaker's words and emotions, and the rhythm of the conversation.

Remember, multitasking might seem like a quick fix, but it's often a shortcut to confusion, errors, and ineffective communication. So, as you go about your day, try to resist the allure of multitasking, especially during conversations. Instead, embrace the power of single-tasking, of focused attention, of truly tuning into the dialogue. It might take some practice, but the rewards—a deeper understanding, stronger connections, and more effective communication—are well worth the effort.

THE ROLE OF PATIENCE AND FOCUS IN ACTIVE LISTENING

Active listening is not a race; it's a marathon. It requires patience and focus, especially when the conversation is long, complex, or emotionally charged. Without these traits, our listening can become superficial, rushed, or ineffective.

Picture yourself learning to play a musical instrument. It's about striking the right notes, but also about the pauses between the notes, the rhythm of the melody, and the focus on each string, each key. Similarly, active listening requires patience to understand the rhythm of the conversation, focus to hit the right notes of comprehension, and techniques to master the melody of understanding.

Let's explore how mindfulness techniques, breathing exercises, the practice of silence, and the power of pause can enhance the rhythm of our active listening.

- **Mindfulness Techniques**

Suppose you're watching a sunset. You're not just observing the changing colors of the sky, but also feeling the wind on your skin, hearing the sounds of the evening, and absorbing the whole experience moment by moment. This is mindfulness, and it's a powerful technique for active listening.

When we practice mindfulness in a conversation, we're fully present in the moment. We're not just hearing the words, but observing the speaker's body language, tone of voice, and emotional cues. We're not planning our response or thinking about our next task, but simply absorbing the conversation as it unfolds.

A simple way to practice mindfulness is to do a quick check-in with yourself during a conversation. Notice your breathing, feel your feet on the ground, register the sound of the speaker's voice. This brief pause can help you refocus your attention and bring you back to the present moment.

- **Breathing Exercises**

Breathing exercises are another useful tool. They can help us stay calm and centered, especially during intense or challenging conversations.

Consider a stressful situation. Your heart is racing, your palms are sweaty, and your mind is buzzing. But then you take a deep breath, and suddenly, things don't seem so overwhelming anymore. That's the power of breathing exercises, and they can be a valuable tool in active listening. These simple techniques, like taking a deep breath *before responding*, can make a big difference in our ability to listen actively.

Deep, mindful breathing can help calm our minds, sharpen our focus, and ground us in the present moment. It's like pressing the reset button, clearing away the mental clutter, and redirecting our attention to the conversation at hand.

A useful breathing exercise you can try is the *4-7-8 technique*. You inhale for a count of four, hold your breath for seven counts, and then exhale slowly for eight counts. This technique can help create a sense of calm and focus, enhancing your ability to listen actively.

- **The Practice of Silence and Pause**

Imagine you're listening to a symphony. The music swells and ebbs, filling the concert hall with sound. But then there's a moment of silence, a pause before the next movement begins. That pause—it's not empty. It's filled with anticipation, with resonance, with meaning. The same applies to conversations. The silences, the pauses, the moments when no one is speaking—these are not voids to be filled. They're spaces for understanding, reflection, and connection. In other words, silence, too, plays a crucial role in active listening. Pausing before you respond gives you time to process what's been said, formulate your thoughts, and respond in a way that adds value to the conversation. It shows the speaker that you're considering their words carefully, that you're not just waiting for your turn to speak but truly seeking to understand their perspective.

Practicing silence in a conversation means resisting the urge to fill every gap with words. It's about being comfortable with pauses, allowing them to add depth and rhythm to the dialogue. It's about understanding that silence can be as meaningful as words, adding richness to the tapestry of our interactions.

So, there we are. Patience and focus, mindfulness and breathing, silence and pauses—these are the beats that add rhythm to the melody of active listening. They're the threads that weave together to form the rich tapestry of understanding, connection, and empathy. As you step forward in your exploration of effective communication, carry these insights with you. They're your guideposts leading you towards the heart of active listening—to understand and be understood, to connect and be connected, to listen and be listened to.

And as you continue on this path, remember this: *communication isn't a monologue*, it's a dialogue. It's not a race, but a dance—a dance of words, of silences, of understanding, and of connection. So, as you navigate your conversations, take a moment to listen, to understand, to connect. Take a moment to dance to the rhythm of active listening. And in doing so, you'll find that you're not just a part of the conversation—*you're a part of the connection, a part of the understanding, a part of the dance.*

And as the rhythm of active listening guides your steps, may your dance be graceful, your understanding deep, and your connections meaningful. For in the end, that's what active listening is all about—it's about turning down the noise, tuning into the melody, and dancing to the rhythm of understanding. And with each conversation, each connection, you're dancing a little bit closer to the heart of communication. So, keep dancing, keep listening, and keep connecting. Your dance floor of understanding awaits.

CLEAR EXPRESSION: SAY WHAT YOU MEAN, MEAN WHAT YOU SAY

*W*hen you are standing in front of a beautiful, intricate painting, you're captivated by the vibrant colors, the delicate brush strokes, the depth and detail of the artwork. Each element on its own is impressive, but together, they create a masterpiece. Now, imagine that each element of this painting represents a component of effective communication. One of the most essential of these elements, the one that brings color and clarity to the painting, is *clear expression*.

THE IMPORTANCE OF CLARITY IN COMMUNICATION

Just like how an artist uses clear lines and vivid colors to bring a painting to life, clear expression can breathe life into our conversations, making them more meaningful and impactful. Let's delve into how clarity in communication can avoid misunderstandings, enhance relationships, boost confidence, and promote transparency.

- **Avoiding Misunderstandings**

Remember playing the game of 'Telephone' as a kid? The message gets distorted as it passes from person to person, leading to hilarious misunderstandings. In real-life communication, however, misunderstandings are far from amusing. They can lead to conflicts, mistakes, and even damage relationships.

By expressing ourselves clearly, we can ensure that our message is understood as intended. It's like providing clear directions to a destination, reducing the chances of the listener getting lost or taking a wrong turn.

- **Enhancing Relationships**

Imagine you're building a puzzle with a friend. If the pieces fit together perfectly, you'll form a beautiful picture. But if the pieces are vague or ambiguous, the picture will be unclear, and the process of building it can become frustrating.

In our relationships, clear communication is like those well-defined puzzle pieces. When we express ourselves clearly, we're able to connect better with the other person, building a stronger, deeper relationship. It's a way of showing respect for the other person's understanding and time, fostering mutual trust and admiration.

- **Boosting Confidence**

Think back to a time when you nailed a presentation or explained a complex concept to someone, and they got it. Didn't it boost your confidence?

When we communicate clearly, it not only helps others understand us better but also boosts our own confidence. It reassures us that we can express our thoughts and feelings effectively. It's like hitting a home run in a baseball game, giving us the confidence to step up to the plate again and again.

- **Promoting Transparency**

Transparency in communication is like a window. It lets in light, allows us to see clearly, and prevents hidden shadows. When we express ourselves clearly, we promote transparency. We let others *see* our thoughts, understand our feelings, and appreciate our intentions.

In personal relationships, transparency builds trust and intimacy. In a professional context, it fosters a culture of openness and collaboration. By expressing ourselves clearly, we're opening the windows to our thoughts and feelings, letting in the light of understanding, and chasing away the shadows of ambiguity.

Clear expression in communication brings clarity to our conversations, adds depth to our relationships, boosts our confidence, and promotes transparency. It's a vital element of effective communication, one that can transform our interactions from mundane to meaningful, from confusing to clear, from estranged to engaging.

Embracing clarity in communication might require practice and patience, but the rewards are well worth the effort. So, as you navigate your conversations, remember to express yourself clearly. ***Say what you mean, mean what you say***, and watch as your conversations transform into masterpieces of understanding, connection, and mutual respect. After all, isn't that the true beauty of communication—the joy of expressing and being understood, the rhythm of speaking and listening, the dance of thought and understanding. So, keep expressing, keep communicating.

THE ROLE OF VOCABULARY: CHOOSING THE RIGHT WORDS

Let's consider the toolbox one more time. You have a variety of tools at your disposal, each designed for a specific task. A hammer for nails, a wrench for bolts, a screwdriver for screws. In communication, our vocabulary is our toolbox, and words are our tools. Each word has its unique function, its distinct purpose. Picking the right word for the right context is a skill that can dramatically enhance our communication.

- **Precision in Language**

When the artists paint, they don't select any blue. They select the perfect shade of blue for the sky in their masterpiece. They select the one that most accurately represents their vision. Similarly, precision in language means choosing the word that most accurately conveys our thoughts, feelings, or ideas.

For instance, saying "I'm happy" is a broad statement. But saying "I'm ecstatic" or "I'm content" paints a more precise picture of your emotional state. Precision in language allows us to express ourselves more accurately, leading to a deeper understanding and a richer dialogue.

- **Avoiding Ambiguity**

Now, imagine you're following a recipe. An instruction like "add a bit of salt" might leave you scratching your head. How much is a bit? A pinch? A teaspoon? A handful? Ambiguity in communication can lead to similar confusion. Words or phrases that are vague or open to interpretation can result in misunderstandings or miscommunication.

To avoid ambiguity, it helps to choose words that are specific and clear. Instead of saying "I'll do it soon," you could say "I'll do it by Friday afternoon." By being specific, you eliminate ambiguity and enhance clarity in your communication.

- **Enhancing Understanding**

Consider a novel that made you lose track of time. The author's choice of words, their way of crafting sentences, their knack for describing scenes so vividly that you felt like you were there—these elements enhance your understanding and enjoyment of the story. In communication, using words that enhance understanding can make our conversations more engaging, relatable, and impactful.

For example, instead of saying "It was a difficult experience," you could say "It felt like climbing a mountain during a storm." This not only enhances the listener's understanding but also makes your message more memorable and impactful.

- **Building Credibility**

In our conversations, using the appropriate vocabulary can enhance our credibility. This doesn't mean using big, complicated words to impress others. It's about using the right words for the context, showing that you understand the topic at hand. Whether it's discussing a book, giving a presentation, or chatting about a hobby, using relevant and accurate vocabulary can boost your credibility and influence in the conversation.

Vocabulary is the toolbox of our communication. Each word, a tool with its unique function. Precision, clarity, understanding, credibility—these are the marks of a well-equipped communicator. By choosing our words wisely, we can bring color, depth, and accuracy to our conversations. We can paint vivid pictures, tell engaging stories, and express our thoughts and feelings with clarity and confidence.

Credibility in communication shows that we know what we're talking about. When we speak with precision and accuracy, we build trust in our listeners. They're more likely to take us seriously, value our input, and engage with us in meaningful dialogue.

For instance, if you're discussing a health issue, using accurate medical terminology can enhance your credibility. Or if you're talking about a book, referencing specific scenes or quotes can show your thorough understanding of the text.

Building credibility is about demonstrating your knowledge and understanding through the accurate use of language. It's about tuning your communication to the right pitch, hitting the right notes to create a harmonious dialogue.

THE ART OF BREVITY: LESS IS MORE

Imagine watching a firework show. Each explosion is breathtaking, filling the sky with color and light. But what if the display just kept going, one firework after another, with no end in sight? Eventually, the awe would fade, replaced by tiredness or even boredom. This is what can happen when we overload our conversations with too much information. The impact of our words gets lost, like those endless fireworks in the sky. That's why, in communication, less is often more.

- **Avoiding Information Overload**

Step into the shoes of a museum curator. Your job is to create an engaging and memorable experience for visitors. You wouldn't display every single artifact in the museum's collection at once. That would be overwhelming, and visitors wouldn't know where to focus. Instead, a good curator selects the most significant pieces, presenting them in a way that tells a compelling story.

The same principle applies to communication. It's about curating your thoughts, selecting the most important points, and presenting them in a clear and concise manner. This helps to avoid information overload, ensuring that your message is digestible and memorable.

- **Enhancing Focus**

Consider a spotlight on a stage. It highlights the main action, drawing the audience's attention to the key elements of the performance. In communication, brevity acts like that spotlight, focusing the listener's attention on the main points.

By keeping your message concise, you help the listener focus on what's important. This enhances their understanding and makes the conversation more engaging. It's like clearing away the clutter on a stage, allowing the main action to shine.

- **Ensuring Message Retention**

Think back to a memorable ad slogan. Chances are, it's short, catchy, and straight to the point. That's because our brains are wired to remember concise and focused information. It's the same reason why phone numbers are broken down into chunks, making them easier to remember.

In conversation, brevity can enhance message retention. By keeping your message concise, you make it easier for the listener to remember your key points. It's like creating a memorable slogan for your ideas, ensuring that they stick in the listener's mind.

- **Promoting Efficiency**

Finally, let's talk about efficiency. Imagine you're running a race. The shortest route to the finish line is a straight line. Any detours or extra steps would slow you down and waste energy. In communication, brevity promotes efficiency. It's about getting to the point quickly and clearly, without unnecessary detours or repetition.

By keeping your message concise, you respect the listener's time and attention. You convey your thoughts efficiently, without wasting words. It's like running that straight line to the finish line, getting your message across in the quickest and most effective way possible.

So, there you have it. Brevity is the art of saying less and meaning more. It's about curating your thoughts, focusing your message, enhancing retention, and promoting efficiency. It's about lighting up the sky with a few well-timed fireworks, creating a display that's memorable, impactful, and beautiful to behold.

As you navigate your conversations, remember the power of brevity. Use it to *spotlight* your main points, to create memorable messages, to respect your listener's time, and to make your communication more effective. And as you do this, you'll find that your conversations become more engaging, memorable, and impactful. Why? Because in the art of communication, less really is more. So, keep practicing brevity. Remember, that it's not just about talking—it's about connecting.

- **Allowing Reflection**

Picture yourself by a quiet lake, the still water reflecting the sky above. It's peaceful, isn't it? In communication, pauses can create a similar sense of peace and reflection. They provide a quiet space for both you and the listener to reflect on what's been said.

Reflection is an essential part of meaningful conversations. It allows us to think deeper, connect the dots, and gain new insights. By adding pauses to our conversations, we create room for this reflection, enriching the dialogue and deepening the connection.

- **Promoting Active Listening**

Finally, let's talk about active listening. It's the art of fully engaging in a conversation, of truly hearing and understanding the other person. And believe it or not, pauses can play a crucial role in promoting active listening.

When we pause, we signal to the listener that we value their attention and response. We show that we're not just interested in talking, but also in hearing what they have to say. It's like passing the ball in a game of catch, inviting them to throw it back. This back-and-forth exchange is the heart of active listening, fostering a sense of shared understanding and mutual respect.

So, there you have it. As you move forward in your daily conversations, remember to use this power of pause. Allow your words to breathe, to resonate, to sink in. And as you do this, you'll find that your conversations become more engaging, more meaningful, and more impactful.

And as you continue to explore the art of effective communication, may you find the melody in the message, the rhythm in the response, and the harmony in the connection.

EXPRESSING YOURSELF CLEARLY: THE ART OF SAYING WHAT YOU MEAN

Think back to a time when you were engrossed in a good book or captivated by a movie. The characters felt real, their experiences resonated with you, and you were hooked on every word or scene. Now, imagine having the same effect during your conversations. This is where the power of storytelling comes into play.

STORYTELLING: A POWERFUL TOOL FOR EXPRESSION

Stories have a way of reaching out and grabbing our attention. They have been a part of human communication since time immemorial, acting as vessels to carry traditions, life lessons, and histories across generations. In our daily interactions, storytelling can turn mundane conversations into engaging dialogues.

- **Creating Relatability**

Let's say you are trying to explain to a friend why it's important to save money. You could shower them with facts and figures, but it might not register. Instead, imagine telling them a story about a person who didn't save money and ended up in a tight spot during an emergency. Instantly, the message becomes more tangible, more relatable.

Stories create a common ground, a shared point of reference. They *humanize* abstract concepts, making them easier to grasp. It's like using a familiar landmark to give directions—it quickly helps the other person understand where they need to go.

- **Enhancing Memory Retention**

Remember the story of the tortoise and the hare from your childhood? How about the tale of Little Red Riding Hood? These stories stick with us because they were memorable narratives, not just dry instructions about life lessons. When we include stories in our conversations, it helps the listener retain the information better.

A story acts like a mental movie, playing out in the listener's mind. This visual element boosts memory retention. It's like attaching a colorful sticky note to an important document—you're more likely to remember it!

- **Building Emotional Connection**

Ever found yourself tearing up while watching a movie? That's because stories have a way of tugging at our heartstrings. They evoke emotions, creating a deeper connection between the speaker and the listener.

When you share personal stories or experiences, you are opening up a piece of your world to the listener. This vulnerability can foster an emotional connection, making the conversation more meaningful. It's akin to inviting someone into your home—it creates a sense of intimacy and closeness.

- **Simplifying Complex Ideas**

Try to explain how a car engine works to someone with no mechanical background. You could use technical jargon and detailed descriptions, but chances are, they would still be confused. Now, consider using a story to explain the same concept, comparing the engine to the human heart, pumping life (or in this case, power) to the rest of the body.

Stories can simplify complex ideas, breaking them down into digestible bits. They provide a framework for understanding, making the unfamiliar, familiar. It's like using training wheels on a bicycle—it helps the rider get the hang of balancing without overwhelming them.

So, the next time you're in a conversation, consider weaving in a story. It could be a personal anecdote, a fictional tale, or even a metaphor. Watch as the listener's eyes light up, their attention captured, their understanding deepened. In communication, stories are the spice that can turn the dish of conversation into a memorable feast. So, go ahead, spice up your communication, and savor the flavors of connection, understanding, and engagement.

ASSERTIVENESS: STANDING UP FOR YOUR THOUGHTS

Assertiveness, in the realm of communication, is like a compass. It points you towards expressing your thoughts clearly, standing up for your beliefs, and navigating interpersonal interactions with confidence. However, it's not about being aggressive or domineering. Rather, it's a balanced way of communication that respects both your rights and those of others. Let's explore the different facets of assertiveness and how it can enhance your communication.

- **Promoting Self-Respect**

Think of assertiveness as your personal advocate. It's a voice that stands up for your interests, needs, and feelings. When you speak assertively, you're acknowledging your worth, asserting your self-respect. Picture it like standing firm on a balancing beam. You're grounded, unapologetic about your space, yet open to others passing by.

By asserting yourself, you're sending a clear message that your thoughts and feelings are valuable. This not only bolsters your self-esteem but also fosters a sense of empowerment. It's like stepping into a spotlight on a stage, illuminating your presence and worth.

- **Encouraging Open Dialogue**

Open dialogue is the lifeblood of healthy communication. It's about creating a space where thoughts and feelings can flow freely, without fear of judgment or criticism. Assertiveness fuels this open dialogue, allowing a river of communication to flow naturally.

When you express yourself assertively, you're inviting others to do the same. You're fostering a communication environment that values honesty, openness, and mutual respect. It's a two-way street where your voice is heard, and so is theirs.

- **Preventing Resentment**

Picture a pressure cooker. Without a vent for steam to escape, the pressure builds up over time, leading to a possible explosion. Similarly, when your thoughts and feelings are continually suppressed, resentment will build up. Assertiveness acts as that vent, allowing your inner pressure to be released in a controlled, constructive manner.

By expressing yourself assertively, you're addressing issues as they arise, preventing the build-up of negative feelings. This not only reduces the risk of conflict but also strengthens your relationships. It's like clearing the air before it gets too heavy, maintaining the lightness and harmony of your interactions.

- **Building Trust**

Trust is the cornerstone of any relationship. It's the solid ground that allows relationships to withstand the storms of misunderstanding or disagreement. Assertive communication plays a vital role in building this trust.

When you communicate assertively, you're transparent about your thoughts and feelings. There's no second-guessing, no hidden agenda. This authenticity fosters trust, as others know that *what they see is what they get*. It's like opening a clear umbrella under a rainy sky. You're shielded, yet your view remains unobstructed.

Assertiveness is your compass in the world of communication. It guides you towards self-respect, open dialogue, reduced resentment, and built trust; ensuring that you stay true to yourself and respectful of others.

So, as you step forward in your communication voyage, remember to pack your compass of assertiveness. Use it to navigate the seas of dialogue, to stand up for your thoughts, to respect the voice of others, and to steer towards clear, confident, and constructive communication. Let this compass guide your words, your silences, your actions, and reactions. And as you do, you'll find that the seas become calmer, the voyage becomes smoother, and the destination of understanding becomes clearer.

Stand up for your thoughts, respect the thoughts of others, and create a map of understanding that others would love to follow. After all, isn't that the essence of effective communication? It's about finding our voice, using it wisely, and creating dialogues that resonate with understanding, empathy, and respect. So, keep communicating, keep exploring, and let your compass of assertiveness guide your way.

THE ROLE OF EMOTION IN EXPRESSION

Imagine a world devoid of color, where everything is in black and white. It would be dull and monotonous, wouldn't it? Now, picture a conversation without emotions. It would lack depth and color, making it just as dull and monotonous. Emotions add vibrancy to our communication, transforming it from a simple exchange of words into a profound sharing of experiences and feelings. Let's explore how emotions play a crucial role in our expression and enhance our communication.

- **Enhancing Connection**

Think about the last time you had a heart-to-heart with a close friend. The conversation probably wasn't just about exchanging facts or ideas. It was about sharing emotions, feelings, and experiences. And it's these shared emotions that enhance the connection between individuals.

When we express our emotions, we invite others to step into our world. We share a piece of ourselves, making the conversation personal and meaningful. It's like opening a window into our soul, allowing others to see our joys, fears, hopes, and sorrows. This emotional vulnerability fosters a deeper connection, making our conversations more engaging and impactful.

- **Promoting Authenticity**

Authenticity in communication is like a beacon of light in the fog. It guides the way, providing clarity and direction. When we express our emotions honestly, we promote authenticity in our communication.

Expressing emotions isn't about putting on a performance or manipulating others. It's about being true to what we're feeling and expressing it in a respectful and appropriate manner. It's about aligning our words with our emotions, ensuring that our external expression matches our internal state. This authenticity not only enhances our credibility but also makes our conversations more meaningful and impactful.

- **Encouraging Empathy**

Have you ever watched a movie and found yourself laughing, crying, or feeling anxious along with the characters? That's empathy in action—our ability to understand and share the feelings of others. In our conversations, expressing our emotions can encourage empathy.

When we share our emotions, we give others a glimpse into our emotional world. This can help them understand our perspective better, fostering empathy. It's like *stepping into their shoes*, experiencing the world from their viewpoint. This shared understanding can enhance the quality of our conversations and strengthen our relationships.

- **Influencing Attitudes and Behaviors**

Remember the last time you watched a motivational speech? The speaker's passion, enthusiasm, and conviction probably stirred something within you, inspiring you to think or act differently. This is an example of how our emotions can influence others' attitudes and behaviors.

When we express our emotions, we're not just sharing how we feel. We're also influencing the emotional climate of the conversation. Our excitement can be infectious, our enthusiasm motivating, our calmness soothing. By being aware of this influence, we can use our emotions to steer the conversation in a positive direction.

So, there you have it. Emotions, the vibrant colors of our communication palette. They transform our conversations from a monochrome sketch into a vivid painting, adding depth, texture, and color.

As you navigate your daily interactions, remember to express your emotions. Let them flow naturally, coloring your conversations with shades of joy, tints of curiosity, hues of excitement, and tones of calmness. Let your emotions be seen, heard, and felt, turning your conversations into masterpieces of connection, understanding, and empathy. And as you do this, you'll find that your conversations become more than just exchanges of words—they become shared experiences, emotional journeys, and meaningful connections.

So, keep expressing, keep feeling, keep sharing. It's not just about talking—it's about feeling. It's about sharing our emotional world with others, inviting them to join us in our joys, our sorrows, our fears, and our hopes.

METAPHORS AND ANALOGIES: YOUR SECRET WEAPONS FOR CLEAR COMMUNICATION

Imagine you're a chef, trying to explain the taste of a new dish to someone who's never tried it. You could list out the ingredients or describe the cooking process, but that might not paint a clear picture. Instead, you might say, "It's like a warm summer day in a bowl" or "Imagine your favorite comfort food, but with a spicy twist." Suddenly, the dish comes alive in their mind. This is the power of metaphors and analogies in communication. Let's take a closer look at how these tools can transform your conversations.

- **Simplifying Complex Concepts**

In our everyday conversations, metaphors and analogies can simplify complex ideas, making them more accessible. They act as bridges, connecting the known with the unknown, the familiar with the new. They help us navigate the complex landscapes of ideas, making our journey of understanding smoother and more enjoyable.

- **Enhancing Understanding**

In our conversations, metaphors and analogies can enhance understanding. They create mental images, helping the listener visualize the message. It's like using a flashlight in a dark room, illuminating the path to understanding.

- **Stimulating Imagination**

Think about reading a novel. The author uses metaphors and analogies to create vivid images in your mind, transporting you to different places and times. For example, "Her eyes were like shimmering pools of moonlight." "The news hit him like a freight train." These phrases stimulate your imagination, making the reading experience more immersive and enjoyable.

In our conversations, metaphors and analogies can stimulate the listener's imagination, making our message more engaging. They add color and texture to our words, turning our conversations into vivid tapestries of ideas and emotions. It's like adding spices to a dish, enhancing its flavor and making it more enjoyable.

- **Creating Impact**

Remember the last powerful speech you heard? Chances are, it was filled with metaphors and analogies. "Life is like a box of chocolates." "All the world's a stage." These phrases pack a punch, leaving a lasting impact on the listener.

Using metaphors and analogies can create a similar impact in our conversations. They make our message more memorable, resonating with the listener long after the conversation ends. It's like leaving a footprint on a sandy beach, marking our presence in the listener's mind.

Metaphors and analogies are your secret weapons for clear communication. They simplify complex concepts, enhance understanding, stimulate imagination, and create impact. They add depth, color, and richness to our conversations, turning them into captivating narratives, engaging dialogues, and memorable exchanges.

As you move forward in your communication journey, remember to wield these powerful tools. Use them to paint vivid images, to strike powerful chords, to tell engaging tales. Let your metaphors and analogies bring your conversations to life, turning your words into symphonies of understanding, bridges of connection, and ladders of insight. And as you do, you'll find that your conversations become more than just exchanges of words—they become shared experiences, emotional journeys, and meaningful connections.

JANET G CRUZ

So, keep expressing, keep connecting, keep creating. It's not just about talking—it's about feeling. It's about sharing our emotional world with others, inviting them to join us in our joys, our sorrows, our fears, and our hopes. So, let your emotions shine, let your feelings resonate, and let your communication be a dance of words and emotions, thoughts and feelings.

PUBLIC SPEAKING - MORE THAN JUST WORDS ON A STAGE

*D*o you remember going to a concert? The lights dimmed, the audience hushed in anticipation; and then, the star of the show steps onto the stage. There's a palpable shift in the atmosphere, an electric charge that zips through the air, connecting each person in the room to the person on stage. That's the power of public speaking. It's not just about talking in front of a crowd; it's about creating a connection, stirring emotions, and making an impact.

Now, I bet you're thinking, "Sounds great, but I'm no rock star." And that's okay! Public speaking is a skill, not a talent, and like any skill, it can be learned, practiced, and honed. In this chapter, we're going to break down the basics of public speaking, from understanding your audience to structuring your speech, using visual aids effectively, and incorporating storytelling techniques.

THE BASICS OF PUBLIC SPEAKING

Public speaking is a lot like cooking. You need the right ingredients (your content), a good recipe (your structure), some garnishing (your visual aids), and a dash of flavor (your storytelling techniques). Let's get cooking!

- **Understanding Your Audience**

Before you start cooking a meal, you need to know who you're cooking for. Are they vegetarians or meat-lovers? Do they have any food allergies? Similarly, before you start crafting your speech, you need to understand your audience.

Who are they? What are their interests, beliefs, and values? What do they already know about your topic, and what do they need to know? These are critical questions to ask because a good speech is not just about what you want to say; it's about what your audience needs to hear.

It's like knowing that your dinner guests are vegetarians and love Italian food. You wouldn't cook a steak; you'd whip up a delicious pasta dish instead. Understanding your audience helps you tailor your speech to their tastes, making it more engaging and impactful.

- **Structuring Your Speech**

Just like a good meal has a starter, main course, and dessert, a good speech has a clear beginning, middle, and end.

The beginning is your appetizer. It should grab your audience's attention, whet their appetite, and make them eager for more. This could be a thought-provoking question, an interesting fact, a personal anecdote, or even a quote that ties in with your topic.

The middle is your main course. This is where you delve into the heart of your topic, presenting your main points in a logical and engaging manner. Use clear, concise language, and break down complex ideas into digestible bits.

The end is your dessert, the sweet finish to your speech. This is where you wrap up your main points, reinforce your message, and leave your audience with a clear takeaway. It could be a call to action, a thought-provoking question, or a powerful statement that encapsulates your speech.

- **Using Visual Aids Effectively**

Visual aids are like the garnish on your dish. They add color, enhance presentation, and make your content more appetizing. Slides, charts, images, or even physical props can serve as visual aids in your speech.

Visual aids should support your speech, not overshadow it. Keep them simple, clear, and relevant to your topic. For example, if you're talking about climate change, a graph showing rising global temperatures can be more impactful than just stating the facts.

Remember, visual aids are tools to enhance your audience's understanding, not crutches for you to lean on. So, use them sparingly and purposefully, just like you would garnish a dish.

- **Incorporating Storytelling Techniques**

Finally, let's add some flavor to our speech with storytelling techniques. Stories are a powerful way to engage your audience, evoke emotions, and make your message more memorable.

You could share a personal story, narrate a case study, or even weave a fictional tale, as long as it supports and enhances your main message. The key is to make your story relatable and emotive, engaging your audience's hearts as well as their minds. Think of storytelling as the secret sauce of your speech. It adds depth, enriches flavor, and leaves your audience wanting more.

DEALING WITH STAGE FRIGHT

Let's talk about elephants. Not the majestic creatures roaming the African savanna, but the one in the room that we often try to ignore - *stage fright*. It's that pesky critter that plants butterflies in our stomach, sends our heart racing, and turns our legs to jelly just when we're about to step onto the stage. But fear not! We're going to tackle this elephant head-on and learn some strategies to keep stage fright in check.

- **Breathing Techniques for Relaxation**

First, let's focus on our breath. Ever noticed how your breathing changes when you're nervous? It often becomes shallow and rapid. By consciously controlling our breath, we can dial down our anxiety and bring our focus back to the present.

Try this simple technique: Inhale slowly and deeply for a count of four, hold your breath for another count of four, then exhale slowly for a count of six. Repeat this a few times and feel your nervousness melt away. It's like a calming mantra for your body, telling it to relax and stay grounded.

- **Visualization Exercises**

Next, let's use the power of our mind. Visualization is a potent tool that can trick our brain into feeling more confident and prepared. Think of it as a mental rehearsal, a sneak peek into a successful performance.

Close your eyes and imagine yourself on the stage, delivering your speech confidently. Visualize the audience nodding, smiling, and applauding. Feel the satisfaction of nailing your speech. The more vividly you can imagine this, the more real it will feel to your brain, and the more confident you'll feel on stage.

- **Positive Affirmations**

Now, let's talk about self-talk. The words we whisper to ourselves, especially in stressful situations, have a profound impact on our feelings and behavior. Positive affirmations are like supportive friends, cheering us on and boosting our confidence.

Choose a few affirmations that resonate with you, like "I am a confident and capable speaker," or "I am calm, collected, and ready to shine." Repeat these to yourself before and during your speech. It's like giving yourself a pep talk, reinforcing your self-belief and calming your nerves.

PRACTICAL TIPS FOR HANDLING NERVES

Finally, here are some practical tips to keep the jitters at bay.

1. **Practice, practice, practice.** Know your material inside out. It's like rehearsing a dance routine until the steps become second nature.
2. **Familiarize yourself with the venue.** Knowing the layout, the acoustics, and the tech setup can help you feel more comfortable on stage.
3. **Warm up your body.** Stretching, jumping jacks, or even a quick walk can help burn off nervous energy.
4. **Smile**. Even if you're not feeling it, the act of smiling can trick your brain into feeling happier and more relaxed.

Remember, stage fright is not something to be eradicated but managed. It's a sign that you care about your performance. With these strategies in your toolkit, you can turn your stage fright into stage might, transforming your nerves into energy, excitement, and enthusiasm. So, take a deep breath, visualize your success, give yourself a pep talk, and step onto that stage with confidence. You've got this!

THE POWER OF PERSUASION: CONVINCING YOUR AUDIENCE

- **Understanding the Principles of Persuasion**

Imagine yourself at a bustling marketplace. The air is thick with the aroma of spices, the chatter of merchants, and the clink of coins. Each merchant is trying to sell their goods, persuading customers to choose them over the others. This marketplace is a lot like public speaking - your words are your goods, and your audience is your customer. Your task? To persuade them to buy into your message.

Persuasion is an art, a subtle dance of influence and understanding. It's not about strong-arming your audience into agreement but about guiding them towards your viewpoint. At the heart of persuasion lie six key principles, as outlined by psychologist Robert Cialdini.

1. **Reciprocity:** People tend to return favors. Give your audience something valuable - a captivating story, a useful insight, a nugget of wisdom - and they'll be more likely to engage with your message.

2. **Commitment and Consistency:** People like to be consistent with their commitments. If you can get your audience to agree to a small point early on, they'll be more likely to agree with larger points later.

3. **Social Proof:** People look to others to decide what to do. Use testimonials, case studies, or statistics to show that others support your message.

4. **Authority:** People tend to obey authority figures. Establish your credibility early on, showing why you're a trusted voice on the topic.

5. **Liking:** People are more likely to be persuaded by people they like. Build rapport with your audience, showing them you're not just a speaker, but a person just like them.

JANET G CRUZ

6. **Scarcity:** People value things that are scarce. Highlight the unique insights or benefits they'll gain from your message, making it feel exclusive and valuable.

These principles are like the spices in the marketplace - blend them skillfully, and you'll create a persuasive feast that your audience will find hard to resist.

- **Crafting a Persuasive Argument**

Next, let's move onto the structure of your persuasive argument. It's like the skeleton of your speech, providing support and shape to your message. A well-structured argument is clear, logical, and compelling, making it easier for your audience to follow along and be persuaded.

Start by stating your position clearly. This sets the stage and gives your audience a clear idea of your stance. Next, present your supporting arguments. These should be strong, compelling points that reinforce your position. Use evidence, like facts, statistics, or expert quotes, to back up each argument. This bolsters your credibility and makes your argument more convincing.

Finally, address potential counterarguments. This shows that you've considered different viewpoints and still stand by your position. Refute these counterarguments logically and respectfully, further strengthening your argument.

Remember, a persuasive argument is not just about what you say, but how you say it. Use clear, concise language, maintain a confident tone, and inject passion into your words. This will make your

96

argument more compelling, resonating with your audience on both a logical and emotional level.

- **Using Rhetorical Devices**

Now, let's add some flair to our speech with rhetorical devices. They add beauty and complexity to your message.

Rhetorical devices can enhance your speech, making it more memorable and impactful. Similes and metaphors can paint vivid pictures in your audience's mind. Repetition can drive home your key points. Rhetorical questions can engage your audience and make them think. Alliteration and rhymes can add a lyrical quality to your speech, making it more enjoyable to listen to.

Use these devices judiciously. Too little, and your speech might be bland. Too much, and it could be overwhelming. Strike the right balance, and your speech will be a flavorful feast that your audience savors.

- **Engaging the Audience Emotionally**

Finally, let's talk about engaging your audience on an emotional level. It's like the heartbeat of your speech, adding life and energy to your words.

Emotions are powerful drivers of action. If you can make your audience feel something - whether it's joy, curiosity, fear, or hope - they'll be more likely to be persuaded by your message. Use stories, anecdotes, or vivid descriptions to evoke emotions. Show your own emotions as well, adding authenticity and passion to your speech.

Remember, a good speech...

1. Doesn't just inform; it inspires.
2. Doesn't just present facts; it paints pictures.
3. Doesn't just speak to the mind; it speaks to the heart.

By engaging your audience emotionally, you're not just delivering a speech; you're *creating an experience*. An experience that informs, inspires, and influences. An experience that they'll remember long after your last word has echoed off the stage.

So there you have it. The art of persuasion in public speaking, demystified. Remember, persuasion isn't about manipulation or coercion. It's about understanding, influencing, and inspiring. It's about speaking not just to people's minds, but also to their hearts. So, as you step onto the stage of public speaking, remember these tools. Use them to craft compelling arguments, engage your audience, and make a lasting impact. The stage is yours. Make your words count.

PRESENTATION SKILLS: BEYOND SPEAKING

Picture yourself at a magic show, watching the magician pull off trick after trick with flair and finesse. The way he moves, the way he speaks, the way he interacts with the audience - it's all part of the act, creating a mesmerizing experience. In public speaking, presentation skills are a lot like that magician's finesse. They're the subtle yet powerful techniques that turn a speech into a performance, a monologue into a dialogue.

- **Effective Use of Body Language**

Let's start with the non-verbal aspect of your presentation - your body language.

Your facial expressions, your gestures, your posture - each plays a vital role in conveying your emotions, emphasizing your points, and engaging your audience. Maintaining eye contact can create a sense of connection and sincerity. Purposeful gestures can add emphasis to your words, making your message more impactful.

But remember, body language can be a double-edged sword. While positive body language can enhance your presentation, negative body language can distract from your message or even create misunderstandings. So, keep your body language open, confident, and aligned with your words. It's like choreographing a dance to match the rhythm of your speech, creating a harmonious performance that captivates your audience.

- **Voice Modulation Techniques**

Next, let's talk about your voice - the instrument you play to deliver your speech. Just like a musician can change the mood of a piece by altering the tempo or dynamics, you can change the impact of your speech by modulating your voice.

Varying your volume can add emphasis to key points and keep your audience engaged. Adjusting your pace can create suspense or convey excitement. Infusing your voice with emotion can make your speech more relatable and impactful. Experiment with these techniques to find the right mix for your style and message. And remember, just like in music, silence can be powerful. Strategic pauses can give your audience time to absorb your words and add drama to your delivery.

- **Engaging the Audience with Questions**

Now, let's turn the spotlight on your audience. A successful presentation is not just about talking; it's about listening too. It's not a monologue; it's a dialogue. And one of the best ways to turn your speech into a conversation is by engaging your audience with questions.

Asking questions invites your audience to actively participate in your presentation. It sparks their curiosity, involves them in your narrative, and makes them feel valued. You could ask for their opinions, test their knowledge, or simply check if they're following along. But remember, if you ask a question, be prepared to listen to the answers. It's about creating a two-way flow of ideas, transforming your presentation into a shared exploration of the topic.

- **Handling Q&A Sessions**

Finally, let's talk about the grand finale of your presentation - the Q&A session. It's like the encore at a concert, giving your audience a chance to interact with you directly and delve deeper into the topic.

Handling a Q&A session requires patience, composure, and quick thinking. Listen carefully to each question, respond honestly, and admit when you don't know the answer. It's okay to pause and collect your thoughts before responding. Remember, the goal is not to show off your knowledge, but to clarify doubts, address concerns, and facilitate understanding.

With these techniques up your sleeve, you can turn your speeches into engaging, impactful, and memorable performances. You can captivate your audience, convey your message effectively, and leave a lasting impression.

Remember, public speaking is not just about delivering a speech; it's about creating an experience. An experience that informs, inspires, and influences. An experience that resonates with your audience long after the applause has faded. So, keep practicing, keep refining, and keep shining on the stage of public speaking. You're not just a speaker; you're a performer, a storyteller, a magician. And the world is eager to hear your story, witness your magic, and join your performance. So, step onto the stage, take a deep breath, and let the show begin.

As we move forward, we'll explore how to communicate effectively across different cultures. It's a small world after all, and our ability to understand and adapt to different cultural norms in communication is crucial. So, stay tuned as we embark on this fascinating exploration of cross-cultural communication.

CULTURAL CONFIDENCE: NAVIGATING GLOBAL COMMUNICATION

*I*magine you're a tourist, lost in a bustling foreign city. The streets are teeming with people, the air is filled with unfamiliar sounds, and the signs are in a language you don't understand. You feel overwhelmed, confused, maybe even a little scared. Now, let's flip the script. Imagine you're in the same city, but this time, you've done your homework. You've learned a few phrases in the local language, familiarized yourself with the customs, and even made friends with some locals. Suddenly, the city doesn't seem so foreign anymore. You feel confident, curious, excited to explore. This is the power of cultural awareness in communication, and in this chapter, we'll learn how to transform that overwhelming foreign city into an exciting adventure.

THE IMPORTANCE OF CULTURAL AWARENESS IN COMMUNICATION

Cultural awareness is like a passport. It opens doors, facilitates connections, and enriches our understanding of the world. But it's not just about knowing facts or learning about customs. It's about understanding, respecting, and adapting to cultural differences in communication.

- **Understanding Cultural Differences**

Think back to that foreign city. Every place has its unique rhythm, its distinct flavor, its own set of unwritten rules. Similarly, every culture has its unique patterns of communication. Some cultures value directness, while others prefer more subtle, indirect ways of expressing thoughts. Some cultures emphasize the individual, while others prioritize the group. Understanding these differences is the first step towards effective cross-cultural communication.

For instance, in some cultures, maintaining eye contact is seen as a sign of respect and attentiveness. However, in other cultures, it may be considered rude or aggressive. By understanding these differences, you can avoid miscommunication and foster better relationships.

- **The Impact of Culture on Communication Styles**

Culture is like the lens through which we view the world. It shapes our perceptions, our behaviors, our communication styles. For example, in high-context cultures like Japan or China, communication is often implicit and indirect, relying heavily on context, nonverbal cues, and shared understandings. In contrast, low-context cultures like the United States or Germany favor explicit, direct communication, where messages are expressed and understood at face value.

Understanding the impact of culture on communication styles can help you adapt your approach when interacting with people from different cultures. It's like switching from driving on the right side of the road to the left - it requires awareness, adaptation, and practice.

- **Recognizing Cultural Stereotypes and Biases**

Stereotypes are like blurry photographs. They provide a vague, oversimplified image, lacking depth and detail. While it's natural for our brains to categorize information to make sense of the world, relying on cultural stereotypes can lead to misunderstandings and biases.

For example, assuming that all Americans are outgoing and straightforward or that all British people are reserved and polite can create false expectations and misinterpretations. Recognizing and challenging these stereotypes is crucial for clear and unbiased cross-cultural communication.

When we embrace cultural awareness in communication, we're not just learning about others - we're learning about ourselves. We're expanding our perspectives, challenging our assumptions, and developing a more nuanced understanding of the world. It's like learning a new language - it's challenging, enriching, and ultimately, empowering. So, as you step into the vibrant marketplace of global communication, remember to pack your passport of cultural awareness. Use it to navigate the bustling streets, connect with the locals, and turn your journey into an unforgettable adventure.

Now, let's continue our exploration of cross-cultural communication by digging deeper into cultural nuances and how to adapt to them. We'll explore decoding non-verbal cues across cultures, adapting your communication style, and navigating language barriers.

UNDERSTANDING AND ADAPTING TO CULTURAL NUANCES

- **Decoding Non-Verbal Cues Across Cultures**

Think of non-verbal cues as the hidden language of cultures, a language that speaks volumes without uttering a word. But like any language, it's subject to interpretation, and these interpretations can vary widely from culture to culture.

Take the simple act of maintaining eye contact. In Western cultures, it's often seen as a sign of confidence and attentiveness. However, in many Asian cultures, prolonged eye contact can be perceived as disrespectful or confrontational. Similarly, the thumbs-up gesture is generally positive in Western cultures, but it can be offensive in some Middle Eastern countries.

The key to decoding these non-verbal cues lies in cultural awareness and observation. It's about being a keen observer, noticing the subtle nuances in people's behavior, and understanding what they imply in a specific cultural context. It's about learning the unspoken rules of the cultural game and playing along.

- **Adapting Your Communication Style**

Adapting to cultural nuances in communication is much like learning to dance to different types of music. Each culture has its rhythm, its tempo, its unique dance steps. And to dance well, you need to tune in to the music, understand its rhythm, and move accordingly.

Your communication style, which includes your choice of words, your tone of voice, your body language, and even your listening habits, is your dance move. And to communicate effectively across cultures, you need to adapt your moves to match the cultural rhythm.

For instance, if you're communicating with someone from a culture that values indirectness and formality, you might need to tone down your usual assertiveness and choose your words more carefully. Conversely, if you're dealing with a culture that appreciates directness and openness, you might need to be more forthright and expressive.

Remember, adapting your communication style doesn't mean losing your authenticity. It's not about mimicking or pretending. It's about being respectful, empathetic, and flexible in your interactions with people from different cultural backgrounds.

- **Navigating Language Barriers**

Language barriers can hinder communication, causing misunderstandings. And while speaking a common language can help, it doesn't guarantee effective communication. Accents, dialects, and cultural idioms can still pose challenges. But with a few strategies, you can navigate these challenges effectively.

1. **Patience is your ally.** Communication might be slower, but that's okay. It's better to take your time to ensure understanding than to rush and risk miscommunication.
2. **Simplicity is your friend.** Avoid using jargon or complex language. Stick to simple words and sentences, and confirm understanding frequently.
3. **Empathy is your guide.** Be understanding and supportive. Encourage the other person to express their thoughts without fear of making mistakes.
4. **Learning is your key.** If you're frequently communicating with people from a specific language background, consider learning some basic phrases in their language. Not only will it help ease communication, but it's also a sign of respect and appreciation for their culture.

Just remember that our goal is not to master every culture's nuances or learn every language. That's an impossible task. Instead, our goal is to cultivate a mindset of cultural sensitivity and adaptability, a mindset that allows us to appreciate cultural differences, adapt our communication accordingly, and build meaningful connections across cultures. After all, at the heart of communication lies connection - the connection of ideas, of feelings, of people from different walks of life. And with cultural confidence, we can strengthen these connections, transforming our interactions into bridges of understanding and respect.

THE ROLE OF RESPECT IN CROSS-CULTURAL COMMUNICATION

- **Showing Respect for Cultural Norms**

Picture yourself as a guest at a traditional tea ceremony in Japan. You observe the meticulous process, the reverence for each movement, the deep-rooted respect for tradition. As a participant, your role isn't merely to sip the tea, but to honor the cultural norms inherent in this ritual. This respect for cultural norms is the bedrock of effective cross-cultural communication.

Every culture has its unique set of norms and etiquette, its unwritten rules that guide social interactions. These can range from how to greet others, how to dress, to more subtle cues like personal space, silence, or indirect communication. In cross-cultural communication, recognizing and respecting these norms is crucial.

It's not about conforming or losing your identity, but about acknowledging and honoring the cultural context in which the communication occurs. It's like learning the steps of a traditional dance. You might stumble initially, but with respect for the tradition and willingness to learn, you can partake in the dance, appreciating its rhythm and significance.

- **Avoiding Offensive Language and Gestures**

In cross-cultural communication, we might unknowingly use language or gestures that are offensive in a different cultural context.

Language, while a powerful tool for communication, is also a cultural construct, laden with nuances and connotations that vary across cultures. A harmless phrase in one culture can be offensive in another. The same goes for gestures. For this reason, it's essential to be mindful of our language and non-verbal cues. When in doubt, it's always better to err on the side of caution, choosing neutral language and gestures.

- **Building Trust Across Cultures**

Think about your closest friends. What makes your bond with them so strong? Most likely, it's trust. Trust is the *glue* that holds relationships together. It's the foundation upon which effective communication is built. In cross-cultural communication, building trust can be a bit more challenging, but it's equally, if not more, important.

Trust in cross-cultural communication is about showing consistency in your words and actions, demonstrating understanding and respect for the other culture, and being open and transparent in your communication. It's about showing up as a reliable, respectful, and empathetic communicator.

To build trust, you should follow through on your commitments, be it a meeting, a deadline, or a promise. It also involves showing empathy and understanding towards cultural differences and viewpoints.

THE POWER OF OBSERVATION IN LEARNING CULTURAL NORMS

Picture yourself as an anthropologist, exploring an uncharted territory. To understand the local culture, you wouldn't just rely on books or guides. You would immerse yourself in the community, observe their way of life, and learn from your experiences. The same approach applies to understanding cultural norms in communication. Let's look at how cultural immersion, observation, and feedback can help us navigate through global communication.

- **Learning from Cultural Immersion**

Think of cultural immersion as a deep dive into a vibrant ocean of customs, traditions, and languages. It's about engaging with the local culture firsthand, experiencing their way of life, their values, their norms. This isn't just about visiting a place; it's about actively participating in local activities, connecting with the people, and embracing their lifestyle.

When you immerse yourself in a different culture, you're not just a spectator; you're a participant. You're not just observing from the sidelines; you're in the thick of the action. This hands-on experience gives you a deeper insight into the cultural nuances of communication, insights that you can't get from books or guides. It's like learning to swim by jumping into the water, not by reading about swimming techniques.

- **Observing and Mimicking Local Communication Styles**

Once you're immersed in a new culture, the next step is to be a keen observer. Pay close attention to how locals interact with each other, how they use verbal and non-verbal cues, how they handle conflicts or disagreements. These observations can give you valuable insights into their communication styles and norms.

But don't just stop at observing. Try mimicking these communication styles in your interactions. It's like learning a dance by watching and copying the moves of a skilled dancer. Initially, you may stumble or feel awkward, but with practice, you'll get the hang of it. Remember, the goal here is not to impersonate or mock the local culture, but to adapt to their communication norms out of respect and understanding.

- **Seeking Feedback and Learning from Mistakes**

No one gets it right all the time, especially when navigating unfamiliar cultural terrains. You're bound to make mistakes, and that's okay. What's important is to learn from these mistakes and use them as stepping stones towards better understanding.

Don't hesitate to seek feedback from locals about your interactions. They can provide valuable insights that can help you improve your cross-cultural communication skills. It's like getting feedback from a dance instructor, helping you refine your moves and improve your performance.

Remember, feedback is a gift, not a criticism. It's a tool for learning, growth, and improvement. So, welcome it with an open mind, use it as a guide for improvement, and appreciate the generosity of those who provide it.

In the vibrant dance of cross-cultural communication, each step you take with awareness, respect, and curiosity brings you closer to the rhythm of unity in diversity. So, keep observing, keep learning, and let your communication be a celebration of diversity, understanding, and respect.

As we move forward, we'll explore how to handle difficult conversations and conflicts, an essential aspect of effective communication.

CONFLICT RESOLUTION: NAVIGATING DIFFICULT CONVERSATIONS

*I*n this chapter, I want you to think of a dam holding back a river. The water builds up, the pressure mounts, and then - if there's no outlet - the dam bursts, causing havoc. In our interactions, unaddressed conflicts or misunderstandings are like that dammed-up river. They build up and can potentially explode, damaging relationships and causing emotional distress. But what if we could create a channel for the river to flow freely? What if we could resolve conflicts effectively, ensuring they don't dam up our relationships? In this chapter, let's explore how we can do just that.

THE CAUSES OF CONFLICT: COMMUNICATION BREAKDOWNS

- **Identifying Common Communication Barriers**

Communication barriers are like potholes on a road. They disrupt the smooth flow of the journey, causing bumps and jolts. In our conversations, these barriers could be anything from misunderstandings and assumptions to differing perspectives and unmet expectations.

For example, imagine you've planned a weekend hiking trip with a friend. You're excited about the adventure, but your friend was looking forward to a relaxed, leisurely walk. This mismatch of expectations could lead to disappointment or even an argument.

Identifying these potholes or barriers is the first step towards smoother conversations. By being aware of potential misunderstandings, making no assumptions, clarifying expectations, and respecting differing perspectives, you can avoid many conflicts right off the bat.

- **Understanding the Role of Emotions in Conflict**

Emotions are like the weather. They can change the landscape of our conversations, turning a sunny chat into a stormy argument. When emotions run high, conflicts can escalate quickly.

Let's say you're discussing a project with a colleague. You're stressed about the impending deadline, and they're frustrated with the workload. Under these emotional clouds, a minor disagreement could quickly turn into a heated conflict.

Understanding the role of emotions in conflict is crucial. When we're aware of our emotional state and that of the other person, we can better manage the conversation. It's like checking the weather forecast before heading out - it prepares you for any storms that might come your way.

- **Recognizing Your Own Conflict Triggers**

Conflict triggers are like buttons. When pushed, they can set off an emotional reaction, leading to conflict. These triggers could be specific words, tone of voice, body language, or even certain topics.

For instance, if you've had a past experience where your ideas were shot down or ridiculed, you might become defensive when your suggestions are questioned. This could trigger a conflict even if the other person had no intention of belittling your ideas.

Recognizing your own conflict triggers is crucial in managing conflicts. By being aware of these triggers, you can mentally prepare yourself for those situations, and *respond rather than react*. It's like having a shield ready to deflect any arrows that might hit those sensitive buttons.

Understanding the common communication barriers can guide us towards effective conflict resolution, ensuring our journey is less about avoiding conflicts and more about resolving them constructively.

TECHNIQUES FOR HANDLING DIFFICULT CONVERSATIONS

- **Active Listening During Conflict**

Facing a storm can be intimidating, especially when that storm is a conflict. Amidst the flashing lightning of accusations and the thundering roars of heated words, it's easy to lose our way. But what if we could calm the storm, one gust at a time? Active listening offers us that calming influence during conflicts.

Active listening guides us through the turbulent waves, helping us navigate the situation with care and understanding. But how does it work exactly?

When engaged in a conflict, instead of preparing your rebuttal or getting lost in your emotions, focus on truly understanding the other person's perspective. Hear their words, observe their body language, and tune into their emotions. It's about giving them your undivided attention, showing that you value their thoughts and feelings.

But active listening isn't just about staying silent; it's about engaging in the conversation. This could be through nods to show you're paying attention, paraphrasing their points to ensure you've understood correctly, or asking clarifying questions to gain deeper insights into their perspective.

Through active listening, you signal to the other person that you're not just there to argue your point, but to understand theirs. This can help de-escalate the conflict, paving the way for a more productive and respectful discussion.

- **Using "I" Statements to Express Feelings**

Using "you" statements during a conflict can distort the other person's perception, making them feel accused or defensive. "I" statements, on the other hand, can bring clarity back into the conversation.

"I" statements bring the focus back on your feelings and perceptions, providing a clear picture of your standpoint. Instead of saying, "You never listen to me," which sounds accusatory; you could say, "I feel unheard when my ideas are dismissed," which focuses on your feelings.

Expressing your feelings using "I" statements helps reduce defensiveness and opens up the space for empathy and understanding. It's like turning down the heat in a simmering pot, preventing it from boiling over.

- **Seeking Win-Win Solutions**

Picture a tug of war. Both sides are pulling as hard as they can, but the rope barely moves. All that effort, and neither side gets what they want. Conflicts can often feel like a tug of war, where both parties are so focused on winning that they lose sight of the possibility of a win-win solution.

Seeking win-win solutions is about dropping the rope and finding a solution that benefits both parties. It's not about compromising or giving in, but about collaborating to find a solution that respects both parties' needs and desires.

This involves brainstorming solutions, discussing each option's pros and cons, and deciding on a solution that both parties are comfortable with. It's like turning that tug of war into a team game, where both parties work together towards a common goal.

In this arena of conflicts, active listening, "I" statements, and seeking win-win solutions are your secret weapons. They help you navigate the battleground with grace, transform conflicts into opportunities for growth, and build stronger, more understanding relationships. So, equip yourself with these tools, step into the arena, and turn conflicts into constructive conversations.

THE ROLE OF EMPATHY IN CONFLICT RESOLUTION

Empathy is like a balm that soothes the sting of conflict. When applied with care, it can ease tension, foster understanding, and mend relationships. However, empathy in conflict resolution is not just about feeling what the other person feels but also about responding in a way that acknowledges their feelings and perspective. Let's explore this further.

- **Understanding the Other Person's Perspective**

We all view the world through our unique lens, shaped by our experiences, beliefs, and values. When conflicts arise, these lenses can color our perception and understanding, leading to misunderstandings and disagreements.

Imagine you're watching a football match with a friend who supports the opposing team. You both watch the same game, but your perspectives are colored by your loyalties. A goal by your team is a moment of joy for you but disappointment for your friend. Understanding this difference in perspective can help avoid unnecessary conflicts.

In the same way, when conflicts arise in our conversations, it's important to look beyond our lens and try to understand the other person's perspective. This might require us to set aside our biases, listen actively, and ask open-ended questions to gain insight into their viewpoint. It's like swapping your football jersey with your friend's and watching the game from their side of the field.

- **Responding with Empathy**

Once we've understood the other person's perspective, the next step is to respond with empathy. This doesn't mean we have to agree with their viewpoint, but we should acknowledge their emotions and validate their feelings.

Imagine your friend is upset because their favorite player missed a crucial goal. You might not share their disappointment, but you can still express empathy by acknowledging their feelings: "That must be really disappointing for you."

In the same way, responding with empathy in a conflict can help de-escalate the situation and foster a more constructive conversation. It's like offering a comforting hand to your friend, acknowledging their disappointment, and letting them know that you're there for them.

- **Rebuilding Relationships After Conflict**

Conflicts, like storms, can leave a trail of damage in their wake. But just as a storm can bring much-needed rain to nourish the earth, conflicts can bring to light issues that need to be addressed, ultimately strengthening the relationship.

Once the conflict has been resolved, it's important to work towards rebuilding the relationship. This might involve discussing what each person has learned from the conflict, brainstorming ways to avoid similar conflicts in the future, and reaffirming your commitment to the relationship.

Rebuilding a relationship after a conflict is like cleaning up after the storm. It requires effort, patience, and a shared commitment to restore balance and harmony. But with time, the sun will shine again, and the relationship can bloom with renewed understanding and respect.

So, there you have it. Empathy in conflict resolution is about understanding the other person's perspective, responding with empathy, and rebuilding relationships after conflict. It's about stepping into their shoes, offering a comforting hand, and working together to restore balance. It's about turning conflicts into opportunities for growth, understanding, and deeper connection.

THE POWER OF APOLOGY: MENDING BROKEN BRIDGES

This time, imagine you're navigating a maze. You're making good progress when suddenly, you hit a dead end. There's no way to move forward. So, what do you do? You backtrack. You return to the point where you made the wrong turn and choose a different path. During conflicts, an apology is like that backtrack. It allows us to return to the point of discord, acknowledge the misstep, and choose a new path towards harmony.

- **Recognizing When an Apology is Needed**

Like a trail marker in the maze, certain signs indicate that an apology is required. Perhaps you've said something hurtful in the heat of the moment, or maybe you've made a mistake that upset the other person. These are clear indicators that an apology is needed.

However, sometimes, the signs are subtler. The other person might seem distant or upset, but you're not sure why. In such cases, it can be helpful to initiate a conversation. Ask if something *you* did upset them. This shows that you care about their feelings and are willing to make amends, even if you're not sure what you did wrong.

Remember, recognizing when an apology is needed is about being attuned to the other person's feelings and being willing to take responsibility for your actions. It's about acknowledging that you've hit a dead end and need to backtrack.

- **Crafting a Sincere Apology**

So, you've recognized that an apology is needed. How do you go about it? An apology is more than just saying "Sorry." It's about expressing regret, taking responsibility, and offering to make amends.

Let's break it down:

1. **Expression of Regret:** This is the "I'm sorry" part. It shows that you understand and regret the impact of your actions.
2. **Explanation of What Went Wrong:** Here, you acknowledge your mistake. Avoid making excuses or blaming others.

3. **Acknowledgment of Responsibility:** This shows that you're taking accountability for your actions.

4. **Declaration of Repentance:** Here, you express your intention to avoid repeating the mistake.

5. **Offer of Repair:** This could be a promise to do better, a gesture of goodwill, or a concrete action to make amends.

6. **Request for Forgiveness:** This part is often overlooked but can be a powerful way to close your apology.

Remember, a sincere apology should be about the other person, not about easing your own guilt or discomfort. It's about acknowledging the hurt you've caused and expressing your genuine desire to make things right.

- **Accepting Apologies Gracefully**

Now, let's flip the scenario. What if you're the one receiving an apology? How can you accept it in a way that promotes healing and reconciliation? Follow these steps:

1. **Acknowledge the apology:** Recognize the courage it took for the other person to apologize and express appreciation for their effort.

2. **Express your feelings:** Share how the incident affected you, but avoid using this as an opportunity to criticize or blame the other person.

3. **Decide whether you're ready to forgive:** It's okay if you need time. Forgiveness is a personal process, and it's important to be honest with yourself and the other person.

Remember, accepting an apology is like finding a new path in the maze, a path that leads towards healing and understanding. It's about allowing both parties to move forward, leaving the dead end behind.

Next, we'll delve into the dynamics of social skills and how they can enhance our interactions. We'll uncover the secrets of building strong social connections through effective communication.

SOCIAL SKILLS: BUILDING BRIDGES, NOT WALLS

*S*ocial skills are your tools for connecting with others, understanding their signals, and maintaining a stable and strong relationship. Let's explore these tools and learn how to set up a seamless social connection.

THE ROLE OF COMMUNICATION IN SOCIAL INTERACTIONS

- **Understanding Social Cues**

Social cues are like the secret language of social interactions. They're the subtle signals that people send out (like a Wi-Fi router), indicating their feelings, intentions, or reactions, and the status of your connection.

Social cues, as we learned in a previous chapter, can be verbal or non-verbal. Verbal cues include things like tone of voice, speed of speech, and choice of words. Non-verbal cues involve body language, facial expressions, and eye contact.

For example, if a friend is speaking quickly and in a high-pitched voice, they might be excited or anxious. If they're avoiding eye contact, they might be uncomfortable or feeling shy. By tuning into these cues, you can understand their emotional state and respond appropriately. It's like adjusting your router settings to ensure a stable connection.

- **Balancing Speaking and Listening**

Communication is a two-way street. It involves speaking your mind and listening to others. It's like the data exchange between your device and the Wi-Fi router. If only one side is active, the connection is incomplete.

When in a conversation, strive for balance. Share your thoughts and feelings, but also give space for the other person to express theirs. Show interest in their views, ask open-ended questions, and listen actively to their responses.

Remember, listening is more than just hearing words. It's about understanding the message, picking up on the emotional undertones, and showing empathy. It's like ensuring your device is sending and receiving data effectively for a seamless online experience.

- **Respecting Personal Boundaries**

In every social interaction, there are invisible lines that we shouldn't cross. These are personal boundaries, the limits that people set to protect their mental, emotional, and physical space. They're like the firewall settings on your router, ensuring a safe and respectful connection.

Respecting personal boundaries involves understanding and accepting the other person's comfort zone. It can be about their personal space, their private life, or their right to disagree.

For instance, if a friend seems uncomfortable discussing a certain topic, it's important to respect that and steer the conversation in a different direction. Or, if a colleague prefers not to mingle at social events, respect their decision without making them feel left out.

In the world of social interactions, understanding social cues, balancing speaking and listening, and respecting personal boundaries are crucial. They ensure a stable, respectful, and meaningful connection with others.

So, the next time you're in a social interaction, remember these tools. Tune into the social cues, strike a balance in your communication, and respect personal boundaries. It's not just about making a connection; it's about making it strong, stable, and secure. Happy socializing!

CHARISMA: THE X-FACTOR IN SOCIAL COMMUNICATION

Let's think of charisma as the secret sauce in your social communication burger. It's that intangible quality that adds a kick to your interactions, making them more engaging, memorable, and impactful. But what exactly goes into this secret sauce? Let's find out.

- **Projecting Confidence**

Confidence is like the foundational layer of your charisma burger. It's the first thing people notice about you, even before you utter a word. But remember, confidence isn't about boasting or showing off. It's about being comfortable in your own skin and believing in your abilities.

When you project confidence, you send out a positive vibe that others find attractive. You command attention and respect, making your interactions more impactful. But how do you project confidence, especially if you're feeling nervous or unsure?

Well, it starts with your body language:

1. **Stand tall, make eye contact, and use open gestures:** This non-verbal communication signals confidence to others.
2. **Pay attention to your voice:** Speak clearly, at a steady pace, and don't forget to breathe. A calm, steady voice implies confidence.
3. **Remember to embrace your uniqueness:** Your unique thoughts, experiences, and perspectives add value to the conversation. So, don't shy away from sharing them. It's about being authentically you, and there's nothing more confident than that.

- **Showing Genuine Interest in Others**

Now, let's add the next layer to our charisma burger - showing genuine interest in others. It's like the juicy patty in your burger that makes people come back for more. When you show genuine interest in others, you make them feel valued and appreciated. This fosters a deeper connection and makes your interactions more engaging.

- **So, how can you show genuine interest? Simple...**

1. **Be curious:** Ask about their interests, their experiences, their opinions.
2. **Listen attentively:** Listen to their responses and respond with thoughtful comments or questions. This shows that you're not just going through the motions, but are truly interested in what they have to say.
3. **Be present:** In our world of constant distractions, giving someone your undivided attention is a powerful way to show interest. So, put away your phone, tune out the background noise, and focus on the person in front of you. It's about making them feel like they're the most important person in the room.

- **Using Humor Effectively**

Finally, let's top off our charisma burger with a dash of humor. Humor is like the tangy sauce in your burger that adds a spark of joy to your interactions. A good laugh can break the ice, lighten the mood, and bring people closer.

But using humor effectively isn't just about cracking jokes or making funny faces. It's about understanding what makes others laugh and adapting your humor to the situation. It's about being playful without being offensive, funny without being inappropriate.

Remember, humor is a powerful tool, but it needs to be used with sensitivity and respect. It's about adding a touch of lightness to your interactions, not at the expense of others' feelings.

So, there you have it - confidence, genuine interest, and humor, the three key ingredients of your charisma burger. Mix them together, and you've got a recipe for social communication that's engaging, memorable, and impactful.

THE ART OF SMALL TALK: STARTING CONVERSATIONS

Think about the last time you bumped into an acquaintance or sat next to a stranger at a social event. The initial exchanges were probably filled with casual, light-hearted banter, the kind we often refer to as 'small talk'. While it may seem trivial or superficial, small talk serves as an essential stepping stone in the process of building deeper connections. It's like dipping your toes in the water before diving in, testing the temperature and getting acclimated. Let's explore how to navigate these initial exchanges and transition smoothly to more meaningful conversations.

- **Finding Common Ground**

In a conversation, finding common ground serves as that firm foundation.

Common ground could be anything - a shared interest, a mutual acquaintance, or even the current weather. It's about finding a topic that both parties can relate to and contribute to. This shared interest or experience provides a safe and neutral starting point for the conversation.

For instance, if you're at a music concert, you could talk about the band, the venue, or your love for music. If you're at a business conference, you could discuss the keynote speech, your professional interests, or your thoughts on the industry trends. The key here is to pick up on cues from your surroundings or from the other person's comments. It's like scanning the field for the most stable patch of land to start building your bridge.

- **Asking Open-Ended Questions**

Once you've found common ground, the next step is to foster dialogue. You can do this by asking open-ended questions. Think of them as the pillars supporting your bridge, allowing the conversation to flow smoothly from one side to the other.

Open-ended questions are inquiries that cannot be answered with a simple 'yes' or 'no'. They encourage the other person to share their thoughts, opinions, or experiences, thereby adding depth to the conversation.

For example, instead of asking "Do you like this band?", which can be answered with a simple yes or no, you could ask "What do you enjoy most about this band's music?" This not only keeps the conversation flowing but also provides insights into the other person's preferences and personality.

- **Transitioning to Deeper Topics**

As the conversation progresses, you might want to steer it towards deeper, more personal topics. This is like extending your bridge further across the field, reaching towards the other side.

Transitioning to deeper topics should be done subtly and respect-fully. Gauge the other person's comfort level and reciprocate their degree of openness. You could share a personal anecdote related to the topic at hand and see how they respond. If they seem comfortable and reciprocate with a personal story of their own, you can gradually steer the conversation towards more profound topics.

Keep in mind that not every conversation will or should reach this stage. The goal of small talk isn't always to dive deep but to connect, engage, and leave a positive impression. It's about building that bridge, whether short or long, to foster under-standing and connection.

So, the next time you find yourself at the start of a conversa-tion, remember these steps.

1. Find common ground.
2. Ask open-ended questions, and
3. Subtly transition to deeper topics.

With these tools, you can transform small talk into meaningful dialogue, building bridges of understanding and connection, one conversation at a time.

BUILDING LONG-LASTING RELATIONSHIPS: IT'S A TWO-WAY STREET

- **Regular Expression of Appreciation: The Secret Ingredient**

Think of your favorite dish. Now imagine it without that secret ingredient that gives it its unique flavor. It just wouldn't be the same, would it? In relationships, expressing appreciation regularly is that secret ingredient. It adds warmth and flavor to your interactions.

So, how can you express appreciation effectively? It's simpler than you might think. It doesn't always have to be grand gestures or lavish gifts. Sometimes, a sincere compliment or a heartfelt "thank you" can make all the difference. It's about acknowledging the other person's efforts, their qualities, or simply their presence in your life.

Remember, appreciation is *a gift that keeps on giving*. It not only makes the other person feel valued but also strengthens the bond between you both. It's like watering a plant regularly, ensuring it grows and thrives.

- **Open and Honest Communication: The Bridge to Understanding**

Open and honest communication guides you through the city of understanding, helping you navigate the streets of emotions, the avenues of thoughts, and the lanes of intentions.

Being open in communication means sharing your thoughts, feelings, and experiences without fear of judgment. It's about being authentic and showing your true self. But remember, being open doesn't mean oversharing or disregarding the other person's comfort level. It's about sharing in a way that fosters connection and trust.

On the other hand, honest communication is about being truthful and sincere. It's about saying what you mean and meaning what you say. But again, honesty doesn't mean being brutally blunt or insensitive. It's about expressing your truth in a kind and respectful way.

Together, open and honest communication builds a sturdy bridge of understanding in your relationships, a bridge that can withstand the weights of disagreements, misunderstandings, and differences.

CONSTRUCTIVE CONFLICT NAVIGATION: TURNING STORMS INTO RAINBOWS

In relationships, conflicts are like storms. They can be daunting, but with constructive conflict navigation, you can turn these storms into rainbows of growth and understanding.

What does it mean to navigate conflicts constructively? It's about dealing with disagreements or misunderstandings in a way that promotes understanding and resolution, rather than further conflict or resentment.

This involves actively listening to the other person's viewpoint, expressing your feelings and thoughts clearly and respectfully, and working together to find a solution or compromise. It's also about knowing when to pause, step back, and cool down if emotions run high.

Remember, conflicts aren't necessarily bad. They're opportunities to learn more about each other, to address issues, and to strengthen your relationship.

Building long-lasting relationships isn't always easy. It requires regular expression of appreciation, open and honest communication, and constructive conflict navigation. It's not a one-time effort but *a continuous process*, like a journey that gets more beautiful with every step. And as you walk this path, you'll find that the destination is worth every effort. Because at the end of the day, it's our relationships that enrich our lives, fill our hearts with joy, and give meaning to our existence. So, keep building, keep connecting, keep cherishing. Because every relationship is a treasure.

With these insights, we are ready to step into the next chapter where we will explore how effective communication can boost your career advancement.

THE POWER OF COMMUNICATION: YOUR KEY TO PROFESSIONAL SUCCESS

*H*ow many times have we heard that communication is key? It's like a mantra repeated across every sphere of life, from personal relationships to professional interactions. But here's the thing - it's not just a cliche; it's the real deal.

Communication is like a swiss army knife in the professional world. It's multifunctional, versatile, and incredibly handy. It's not just about getting your point across; it's about building relationships, demonstrating leadership, navigating office politics, and so much more. Let's get down to the nitty-gritty of how effective communication can pave the way for professional success.

THE ROLE OF EFFECTIVE COMMUNICATION IN PROFESSIONAL SUCCESS

- **Building Professional Relationships**

Remember the first day of school? A room full of unfamiliar faces, a whirlpool of emotions, and a burning desire to make friends. Now, fast forward to your professional life. Isn't it somewhat similar? You step into a new job or a new project, surrounded by colleagues, clients, or stakeholders, and your ability to build relationships can make all the difference.

Effective communication is like the cement that holds the bricks of professional relationships together. It's about exchanging ideas, sharing feedback, and collaborating towards common goals. It's about active listening, understanding different perspectives, and responding with empathy and respect.

For instance, consider a situation where you're working on a team project. The ability to clearly express your ideas, listen to your team members' inputs, and collaborate efficiently can foster a positive working environment. It can boost team morale, enhance productivity, and strengthen your professional relationships.

- **Demonstrating Leadership Through Communication**

Imagine watching a symphony orchestra. The conductor, with a simple wave of the baton, guides the musicians, ensuring harmony in their performance. In the professional world, effective communication is like that baton, a tool that can guide, inspire, and lead.

Whether you're a team leader, a manager, or a CEO, your ability to communicate effectively can significantly impact your leadership. It's about setting clear expectations, providing constructive feedback, and motivating your team. It's about expressing your vision, aligning your team's efforts, and fostering a culture of open communication.

For example, let's say you're leading a product development team. Your ability to clearly communicate the project goals, articulate the roles and responsibilities, and address any concerns or questions can facilitate a smooth execution of the project. It can also enhance your team's trust in your leadership, fostering a sense of unity and collaboration.

- **Navigating Office Politics**

Office politics it's like walking through a minefield. One wrong step, and boom! But here's the good news. Effective communication can be your map in this minefield, helping you navigate with finesse.

Office politics often stem from miscommunication, misunderstandings, or conflicting interests. Effective communication can help address these issues head-on, reducing friction and fostering a positive work environment.

It's about being transparent, addressing issues constructively, and promoting open dialogue. It's about understanding the dynamics, acknowledging different viewpoints, and facilitating solutions.

Let's take an example. Suppose there's a disagreement in your team regarding the allocation of resources for a project. Instead of taking sides or avoiding the issue, you can facilitate an open discussion where each team member can express their viewpoint. By promoting open dialogue and seeking a mutually beneficial solution, you can navigate the situation effectively, turning potential conflicts into opportunities for collaboration.

To sum it up, effective communication in the professional sphere is like a powerful engine that drives success. Whether it's building robust professional relationships, demonstrating leadership, or navigating office politics, effective communication plays a pivotal role. It's the golden thread that weaves together the fabric of professional success. So, let's harness the power of communication and unlock our professional potential.

NETWORKING: BUILDING PROFESSIONAL RELATIONSHIPS

Networking - the term might conjure images of stuffy business events, awkward introductions, and forced small talk. But let's flip the script. Think of networking as a vibrant marketplace, bustling with opportunities to connect, learn, and grow. It's a dynamic space where ideas meet minds, needs meet solutions, and people meet potential. So, how do we navigate this marketplace effectively? Let's break it down.

- **Making a Positive First Impression**

When you go to a gallery, the first artwork you see sets the tone for your entire visit. It captures your attention, sparks your curiosity, and draws you into the world of art. Similarly, in the gallery of networking, your first impression is that artwork. It's your initial showcase, your hook that draws people in.

Making a positive first impression isn't just about dressing sharply or flashing a charismatic smile - although those certainly don't hurt! It's about projecting confidence, showing genuine interest, and engaging in meaningful conversation.

When you meet someone for the first time, introduce yourself clearly and warmly. Be attentive, maintain eye contact, and show enthusiasm in your body language. Engage in the conversation, ask insightful questions, and listen actively to their responses. Remember, your goal is not just to impress, but to express your authenticity, your interest, and your value.

- **Following Up After Networking Events**

Imagine you've collected a handful of intriguing business cards from a networking event. They're sitting on your desk, reminders of interesting conversations and potential connections. But as time passes, these cards gather dust, and the connections fade away. Sounds familiar?

The good news is, it doesn't have to be this way. Following up after networking events is like watering the seeds you've planted. It nourishes the potential connections, transforming them into thriving relationships.

Reach out to the people you've met, preferably within a week of the event. A simple email or LinkedIn message can do the trick. Recap your conversation, express your interest in keeping in touch, and suggest a follow-up meeting if appropriate.

Remember, the goal of networking is not just to collect contacts; it's to build connections. And these connections need nurturing to grow. So, don't let those business cards gather dust. Follow up, reach out, and watch your professional network flourish.

- **Building a Professional Network Online**

Welcome to the digital age, where networking doesn't require a suit, a business card, or even a physical presence. Online platforms like LinkedIn, Twitter, and industry-specific forums provide ample opportunities to build and expand your professional network.

Online networking is like exploring a new city through Google maps. It offers a bird's eye view of the professional landscape, allowing you to navigate and connect with ease.

Start by creating a compelling online profile. Highlight your skills, experiences, and aspirations. Join relevant groups, participate in discussions, share insightful content, and connect with professionals in your field.

While online networking provides convenience and reach, it also requires etiquette and caution. Be respectful, professional, and authentic in your interactions. Avoid spamming, oversharing, or infringing on others' privacy.

In the grand arena of professional life, networking is not just a strategy; it's a skill, one that can open doors, create opportunities, and foster lasting relationships. So, whether you're making a first impression, following up after an event, or networking online, remember - every interaction is a chance to connect, to learn, and to grow. So, get out there, start connecting, and let your professional network be your springboard to success.

THE ART OF PERSUASION: GETTING YOUR IDEAS ACROSS

- **Crafting a Compelling Argument**

Let's assemble a puzzle. You start with the corners and edges, gradually filling in the middle until a complete picture forms. Much like this, crafting a compelling argument requires a similar approach. You start with your main idea, gradually building on it with supporting points until a comprehensive argument forms.

The foundation of your argument is your main idea or claim. This should be clear, concise, and debatable. It's like the corner piece of your puzzle, providing the starting point for the rest of your argument.

Next, you add your supporting points. These are the reasons or evidence that back up your main idea. Each supporting point should be strong enough to stand on its own, yet collectively, they should create a cohesive argument. They are the edge pieces of your puzzle, framing and supporting your main idea.

Finally, you tie everything together with a clear line of reasoning. This is the logical progression that connects your main idea with your supporting points. It's like the middle pieces of your puzzle, filling in the gaps and completing the picture.

Remember, a compelling argument is not just about what you say, but *how you say it*. Use confident and persuasive language, maintain a logical structure, and stay focused on your main idea. It's like carefully placing each piece of the puzzle to create a clear and captivating picture.

- **Using Evidence to Support Your Ideas**

In a court case, the verdict often hinges on the strength of the evidence. Similarly, in persuasion, the impact of your argument depends on the quality of your evidence.

Evidence comes in various forms - facts, statistics, examples, testimonies, and more. It's like the fuel that powers your argument, giving it strength and credibility. But remember, not all fuel is created equal. High-quality evidence is accurate, relevant, and credible.

1. **Accurate evidence** is factually correct. It's like using the right type of fuel for your engine; it ensures your argument runs smoothly without any hiccups.
2. **Relevant evidence** directly supports your main idea. It's like using the right amount of fuel; too much or too little can hamper the performance of your argument.
3. **Credible evidence** comes from reliable sources. It's like using clean fuel; it boosts the performance of your argument and prevents any damage to its credibility.

So, when you're building your argument, remember to fuel it with high-quality evidence. It's the power source that drives your argument towards the destination of persuasion.

- **Handling Objections Gracefully**

Imagine you're sailing a boat. Suddenly, you encounter a wave. Do you panic and abandon ship? Of course not. You ride the wave, adjusting your course as needed. Similarly, when you encounter objections in persuasion, you don't abandon your argument. You handle them gracefully, adjusting your course as needed.

Handling objections involves three steps - acknowledging, understanding, and responding.

1. **Acknowledging the objection** shows that you respect the other person's viewpoint. It's like spotting the wave from a distance; it's the first step towards navigating it successfully.

2. **Understanding the objection** involves actively listening to the other person's concerns and seeking clarification if needed. It's like gauging the size and speed of the wave; it helps you determine the best course of action.

3. **Responding to the objection** involves addressing the concerns raised, either by providing additional evidence, offering a counter-argument, or modifying your original argument. It's like adjusting your boat's direction and speed; it helps you navigate the wave without capsizing.

Remember, objections are not roadblocks; *they're opportunities for further discussion and deeper understanding.* They challenge you to strengthen your argument and improve your persuasion skills. It's like riding the wave; it might be challenging, but it also makes the journey more exciting and rewarding.

FEEDBACK: THE ECHO IN THE COMMUNICATION CANYON

Feedback is like an echo in the communication canyon. It bounces back, providing a valuable reflection of our words, actions, and impact. It's a tool for growth, a mirror for self-awareness, and a compass for improvement. Let's decode this echo and understand how to give and receive feedback effectively.

- **Constructive Feedback Techniques: Building, Not Breaking**

Imagine you're crafting a sculpture. You chip away, piece by piece, shaping the raw stone into a work of art. Giving constructive feedback is somewhat similar. It's about chipping away at the rough edges, helping the other person shape their skills and performance into something better.

Constructive feedback is more than just pointing out mistakes or shortcomings like some people do. It's about providing specific, actionable, and balanced insights that can help the other person improve. Here's how to do it right:

1. **Be Specific:** General comments like "good job" or "needs improvement" are like blurry road signs. They don't provide a clear direction. Instead, pinpoint the exact behavior or result that you're addressing.
2. **Focus on Behavior, Not Personality:** Feedback should be about what the person does, not who they are. It's about their actions, not their character. This keeps the feedback objective and prevents it from becoming personal.
3. **Be Balanced:** Constructive feedback is not just about highlighting the negative. It's also about acknowledging the positive. It's like a balanced meal, nourishing growth with a mix of encouragement and improvement.
4. **Make It Actionable:** Feedback should provide a clear path to improvement. Offer concrete suggestions or steps that the person can take to improve. It's like a roadmap, guiding the journey of growth.

- **Receiving Feedback with Grace: A Gift, Not a Grenade**

What happens when you receive a gift? You accept it graciously, regardless of whether you like it or not. Receiving feedback is somewhat similar. It's a gift of insight, an offering of growth. And just like a gift, it's not always wrapped in shiny paper or tied with a pretty bow. But with grace and openness, you can unwrap its value.

Here's how to receive feedback with grace:

1. **Listen Actively:** Before responding to feedback, make sure you fully understand it. Listen attentively, ask clarifying questions if needed, and resist the urge to interrupt or defend yourself immediately.
2. **Consider the Intent:** Remember, feedback is meant to help you improve, not to belittle or criticize you. It's a gift of insight, not a grenade of negativity.
3. **Respond, Don't React:** Take a moment to process the feedback before responding. This helps you respond thoughtfully rather than react defensively.
4. **Say Thank You:** Regardless of whether you agree with the feedback, thank the person for their input. It shows that you value their perspective and appreciate their effort to help you improve.

USING FEEDBACK FOR CONTINUOUS IMPROVEMENT: THE CYCLE OF GROWTH

Imagine a cycle. It moves forward, not in a straight line, but in a circular motion. The wheels rotate, propelling the cycle forward. I believe we can say that continuous improvement is similar to a rotating wheel when it's fueled by feedback. It's a cycle of growth, propelled by the rotation of action, feedback, and improvement.

Here's how to use feedback for continuous improvement:

1. **Reflect:** Take some time to reflect on the feedback. What are the key insights? What can you learn from it?
2. **Plan:** Based on your reflection, make a plan for improvement. Identify specific actions you can take to address the feedback.
3. **Act:** Implement your plan. Put your improvement actions into practice.
4. **Seek Feedback Again:** After implementing your actions, seek feedback again. Has your performance improved? What further improvements can you make?

This cycle of reflection, planning, action, and feedback creates a continuous loop of learning and growth. It's like pedaling a cycle; each rotation propels you forward and each feedback propels your growth.

Feedback is the echo in communication that guides our path, shapes our growth, and enhances our performance. Whether we're giving or receiving feedback, or using it for continuous improvement, it's a powerful tool for professional success. With this echo as our guide, we're not just communicating; we're actually connecting, we're growing, we're succeeding. So, let's keep the echo alive, let's keep growing, and let the canyon of our professional life resonate with the echoes of success.

With these communication skills in our toolkit, we're ready to explore another critical aspect of communication - *the written form.* In the next chapter, we'll dive into the world of effective written communication and its impact on personal and professional success.

THE EVER-EVOLVING ROADMAP
OF COMMUNICATION MASTERY

*I*n this chapter, you're an adventurer, standing at the edge of a vast, unexplored jungle. With every step you take, you discover a new plant, a new animal, a new path. The thrill is in the unknown, in the continuous discovery, in the constant learning. Communication, my friend, is that vast, unexplored jungle, and you are that adventurer. With every conversation, every interaction, every connection, you learn something new, you discover a different path, and you grow as a communicator.

THE ROLE OF CONTINUOUS LEARNING IN COMMUNICATION SKILLS

- **Seeking Opportunities for Growth**

As an adventurer, you don't just wait for a new discovery to fall into your lap. You actively seek it out. Similarly, improving your communication skills involves actively seeking opportunities for growth.

This could be by participating in a public speaking workshop, reading a book on emotional intelligence, or even by practicing active listening in your daily conversations. It's about stepping out of your comfort zone and embracing every opportunity as a learning experience.

Remember that memorable family reunion where Uncle Bob narrated his travel tales? That was an opportunity for you to observe storytelling skills. How about that group project at work where you coordinated with different departments? That was an opportunity for you to practice negotiation and conflict resolution. Opportunities for growth are all around us; we just need to recognize and seize them.

- **Learning from Mistakes**

Every adventurer knows that the path to discovery is littered with mistakes and missteps. But these mistakes are not roadblocks; they're stepping stones. They're opportunities to learn, to grow, to improve.

In communication, mistakes are inevitable. Maybe you said something that was misinterpreted, or perhaps you didn't listen as actively as you could have. Instead of beating yourself up over these mistakes, use them as a learning tool. Reflect on what went wrong, understand why it happened, and identify what you can do differently next time.

Let's say you cracked a joke at a team meeting that didn't land well. Instead of dwelling on the awkward silence that followed, take a moment to understand why the joke didn't work. Was it inappropriate for the situation? Was it delivered with the wrong tone? Learning from this experience can help you hone your sense of humor in the future to be more aligned with your audience.

- **Staying Updated with Communication Trends**

The jungle of communication is ever-evolving. New paths emerge, old paths disappear, and the landscape keeps changing. Staying updated with the latest communication trends is like having a map that evolves with the jungle. It's progress.

This could involve understanding the latest research in communication psychology, getting updated with new cultural nuances in global communication, or even familiarizing yourself with the trending slang in digital communication.

For example, with the rise of remote work, virtual communication has become a trend that's here to stay. Embracing this trend could involve understanding the nuances of video calls, mastering the art of digital body language, or even learning how to write effective emails.

In the ever-evolving jungle of communication, being a continuous learner is not an option; it's a necessity. It's the only way to navigate this changing landscape, to discover new paths, and grow as a communicator. So, keep seeking opportunities for growth and, keep learning from your mistakes. Keep updating yourself with the latest trends. The jungle is vast, the possibilities are endless, and the thrill of discovery is unparalleled. Enjoy exploring!

BUILDING YOUR PERSONAL COMMUNICATION STYLE

I also compare conversation with a dance. If you think about it, each person has their unique rhythm and their distinctive moves, but magic happens when these rhythms blend, creating a dance that's engaging and harmonious. Your communication style is that unique rhythm. It's your signature dance move that sets you apart in the grand dance hall of communication. Let's explore how you can build your personal communication style, one step at a time.

- **Understanding Your Communication Strengths and Weaknesses**

The first step in building your personal communication style is also similar to sculpting. You will be the sculptor. It involves chipping away at your communication habits to identify your strengths and weaknesses.

Your strengths are the finer details of your communication style, the elements that you naturally excel at. Maybe you're a great listener, or perhaps you're skilled at expressing your thoughts clearly. These strengths are the building blocks of your personal communication style.

On the other hand, your weaknesses are the rough edges that need some smoothing. Perhaps you tend to interrupt others, or maybe you struggle with public speaking. These are the areas where you have the opportunity to improve and grow.

- **Developing Your Unique Voice**

The next step is to develop your unique voice once you've identified your strengths and weaknesses. This is your distinctive tone, your personal touch that sets your communication style apart from others.

Your unique voice is a reflection of your personality, your values, and your experiences. It's about expressing yourself authentically, being true to who you are. But remember, finding your voice isn't about putting on a performance. It's about being real, being you.

To develop your unique voice, pay attention to how you naturally communicate when you're relaxed and comfortable. Notice your choice of words, your tone, your body language. Experiment with different ways of expressing yourself, and see what feels most authentic to you.

- **Adapting Your Style to Different Situations**

A skilled communicator can *adapt* their style to different situations. This is the final step in building your personal communication style.

Adapting your communication style involves understanding the context, considering the other person's communication preferences, and adjusting your approach accordingly. It's not about changing who you are, but about adjusting your dance moves to match the rhythm of the situation.

For instance, a formal business meeting might require a more structured and professional communication style. On the other hand, a casual chat with a friend might allow for a more relaxed and informal style. By adapting your style to different situations, you ensure that your communication is effective and appropriate all the time.

THE IMPORTANCE OF REFLECTION AND SELF-EVALUATION

We often rush from one task to the next in our daily lives, rarely pausing to take a breather. Just like a hamster on a wheel, we keep running, but do we ever stop to check if we're on the right track? This is where reflection and self-evaluation step in. They're like a pit-stop in a marathon, a checkpoint in a race. They allow us to pause, assess, and adjust our course as needed. Let's explore how these pit-stops can boost our communication skills.

- **Regular Self-Assessment of Communication Skills**

In this section you are going to play basketball. After every game, you analyze your performance, identifying what worked and what didn't. This analysis is a crucial part of your practice, steering your progress and sharpening your skills. Similarly, regular self-assessment is an integral part of honing your communication skills.

Self-assessment is like a personal scorecard that allows you to evaluate your communication abilities objectively. How effectively did you convey your thoughts in the last team meeting? Did you listen actively during your conversation with a friend? Were you able to handle the disagreement with your partner constructively?

By asking such questions, you can identify your strengths and areas for improvement. This evaluation is not about judging yourself harshly but about understanding your communication patterns. It's like checking your basketball stats, not to criticize, but to improve.

- **Seeking Feedback from Others**

Now, imagine you're practicing your basketball shots, and a seasoned player offers you some tips. This external feedback is invaluable, providing a fresh perspective and expert insights. In the world of communication, seeking feedback from others serves a similar purpose.

You don't need feedback only in professional communication like we discussed in the previous chapter. Feedback reflects how your words and actions are perceived by others in your personal life too. It's like a mirror. It provides an outside perspective that complements your self-assessment.

For instance, you might feel that you're a good listener, but your friend might point out that you often interrupt when others are speaking. This feedback doesn't mean you're a bad listener; it simply highlights an area you might not have noticed and can work on.

Remember, when seeking feedback, choose someone you trust and respect. Be open to their insights, and take their suggestions in a positive stride. It's not about pleasing everyone; it's about understanding different perspectives to enrich your communication skills.

- **Setting Goals for Improvement**

Back to the basketball court. Once you've analyzed your stats and received tips from the seasoned player, what's the next step? You set goals for improvement. You identify specific areas you want to work on and create a plan to achieve those goals. In communication, setting goals for improvement follows a similar path.

Setting communication goals provides a clear direction, marking the waypoints for your progress. These goals could range from enhancing your active listening skills, improving your body language, to handling conflicts more constructively.

Once you've set your goals, break them down into actionable steps. If your goal is to improve active listening, an actionable step could be practicing reflective listening in your daily conversations. Keep these steps realistic and achievable, and celebrate your progress along the way.

Remember, improving communication skills is not a destination; *it's a process, a constant evolution.* By setting goals for improvement, you're not just marking the finish line; you're actually charting the course for your ongoing journey. So, set your goals, lace up your shoes, and get ready for the marathon. It's not about winning the race; it's about enjoying the run, one stride at a time.

Reflection and self-evaluation will be your faithful companions to master the art of communication. They will guide your path, fuel your progress, and enrich your journey. So, take that pit-stop, reflect on your performance, and set your goals.

EMBRACING CHANGE: ADAPTING YOUR COMMUNICATION STYLE

- **Recognizing When Change is Needed**

We often encounter signs in the form of recurring misunderstandings, unproductive arguments, or simply a feeling of being unheard or misunderstood that are telling us something has to change.

These signs indicate that your current communication style may not be fully effective, and it might be time to experiment with a different approach. Perhaps you've been relying too heavily on email or texting for important discussions when a face-to-face conversation could be more effective. Or maybe you've been holding back your opinions for fear of conflict when expressing them assertively could lead to better outcomes.

Recognizing the need for change is the first step towards enhancing your communication skills. It's about being aware, being adaptable, and being ready to steer your communication in a different way.

- **Being Open to New Communication Techniques**

Once you've recognized the need for change, the next step is to be open to new communication techniques. This is like being willing to try a different route, a new mode of transport, or even a fresh perspective on your journey.

Being open to new techniques involves learning from various sources - books, workshops, online courses, mentors, or even the people around you. It's about acknowledging that there's always something new to learn in the vast landscape of communication.

For instance, you could explore the technique of nonviolent communication to express your needs without triggering defensive reactions. Or you might experiment with the use of storytelling to make your presentations more engaging. Embracing new techniques is like adding new tools to your communication toolkit, equipping you to navigate various situations more effectively.

- **Embracing Technological Advances in Communication**

In today's digital age, technology plays a significant role in how we communicate. From emails and video calls to social media and instant messaging apps, technological advances have transformed the way we connect with each other.

Embracing these technologies can enhance your communication skills and expand your reach. For example, using video calls for remote meetings can provide the benefits of face-to-face interaction, even when you can't be in the same location. Similarly, using collaborative online tools can make team projects more efficient and inclusive.

However, it's also important to navigate the challenges posed by technology, such as the risk of miscommunication in text messages or the lack of personal connection in virtual interactions. Balancing the use of technology with the need for personal, meaningful communication is key to effective communication in the digital age.

In the ever-evolving landscape of communication, change is the only constant. Whether it's recognizing the need for change, being open to new techniques, or embracing technological advances, adapting your communication style is key to staying effective and relevant.

So, as you continue to venture down the road of communication, remember to be flexible, be open, and be willing to change. It's not just about reaching the destination; it's about enjoying the ride, embracing the detours, and appreciating the scenery along the way.

CONCLUSION

*A*lright, we've journeyed a long way together. From the basics of verbal and non-verbal communication to mastering the art of public speaking, from navigating tricky office politics to building a personal communication style - you've tried it all. You've been brave, you've been curious, and you've been patient. Now, it's time to reflect on this journey and look ahead.

Think about how your understanding of communication has evolved. Remember the "aha" moments, the challenges, the breakthroughs. Take a moment to pat yourself on the back for all the progress you've made. You've not just read a book; you've embarked on a journey of self-discovery, growth, and empowerment.

Now that you're armed with these new skills, it's time to take them out into the real world. Use active listening in your next team meeting. Try out your storytelling skills with your family.

Stand up for your ideas with assertiveness. Each day is a new opportunity to practice and polish these skills.

Remember, learning is a lifelong journey, especially when it comes to communication. So, keep reading, keep exploring, keep experimenting. Don't be afraid of making mistakes - they're your best teachers. Stay open to feedback and keep refining your skills.

As you grow, don't forget to share your journey with others. Inspire your friends, your colleagues, your loved ones with your communication skills. Show them it's possible to say what you mean, mean what you say, and still be kind and respectful. Be the beacon of effective communication in a world that so desperately needs it.

Looking forward, imagine a world where misunderstandings are rare, where people listen to understand, where differences in opinion lead to constructive dialogues instead of conflicts. Sounds like a dream, right? But guess what - you are now part of making this dream come true, one conversation at a time.

So, go out there and use your words to connect, to understand, and to inspire. And remember, the power of effective communication is now in your hands. Hold it with care and wield it with confidence. Here's to a future filled with meaningful conversations and deep connections.

Happy communicating!

LEAVE A 1-CLICK REVIEW

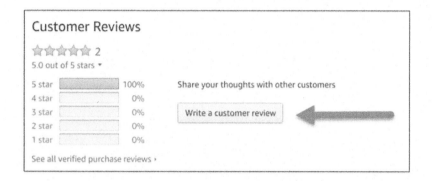

I would be incredibly thankful if you take just
60-seconds to write a brief review on Amazon,
even if it's just a few sentences!

https://shorturl.at/bilwN

ABOUT THE AUTHOR

Janet C. Cruz is the author of several self-help books. She brings a unique blend of expertise to the realm of communication and effective listening. With a strong academic foundation in psychology and sociology, she possesses a deep understanding of human behavior and social dynamics.

With her collection of books, the author aims to empower readers by providing tools and strategies for personal growth. Whether it's about cultivating positive habits, overcoming mental obstacles, or finding happiness, these books offer guidance that readers can apply to their own lives.

Some of her publications include:

- **The Dementia Caregiver's Survival Guide:** An 11-Step Plan to Understand the Disease and How to Cope with Financial Challenges, Patient Aggression, and Depression Without Guilt, Overwhelm, or Burnout. (English and Spanish editions)

- **Dementia Caregiving:** A Self-Help Book for Dementia Caregivers Offering Practical Coping Strategies and Support to Overcome Burnout, Increase Awareness, and Build Mental & Emotional Resilience.

- **Caring for Aging Parents:** Step-by-Step Guide to Navigating the Challenges and Embracing the Blessings of Caring for Your Parents.

- **Developing Drug Addiction Recovery Skills by Understanding Addiction and The Brain:** The Ultimate Guide to Build Resilience to Prevent Relapse.

BIBLIOGRAPHY

GoodTherapy. (2020). *Nonverbal Communication* Retrieved From. https://www.-goodtherapy.org/blog/psychpedia/nonverbal-communication

Segal, J, PhD, Smith, Melinda, M.A., Robinson, L., Boose, G. (2023). *Nonverbal Communication and Body Language.* Retrieve From. https://www.helpguide.org/articles/relationships-communication/nonverbal-communication.htm

Drake, Kimberly. (2022). *Silent Communication: Effectiveness, Importance, and Tips.* Retrieve From. https://psychcentral.com/relationships/silent-communication

Brewer, T., PhD. (2033). *For Effective Communication Tone (Surprise!) Matters Most.* Retrieved From. https://www.forbes.com/sites/tracybrower/2023/02/26/for-effective-communication-tone-surprise-matters-most-5-strategies-for-effec-tiveness/

MindManager. (2012). *Communication Breakdown: Left Brain vs. Right Brain.* Retrieved From. https://blog.mindmanager.com/communication-breakdown-left-brain-vs-right-brain/

Doshi, P. (2022). *Effective Communication Skills Start With Emotional Intelligence.* Retrieved From. https://trainingindustry.com/articles/professional-develop-ment/effective-communication-skills-start-with-emotional-intelligence/

ParadoxMarketing. *How Perception Influences Interpersonal Communication.* Retrieved From. https://paradoxmarketing.io/capabilities/customer-market-ing/insights/how-perception-influences-interpersonal-communication/

HumanMetrics. *Communication Strategies for Different Personality Types.* Retrieved From. https://www.humanmetrics.com/personality/communication-strate-gies-for-different-types

The Mind Tolls Content Team. *Active Listening - Hear What People are Really Saying.* Retrieved From. https://www.mindtools.com/az4wxv7/active-listening

Council, A., MA. (2022). *Active Listening: Techniques, Benefits, Examples.* Retrieved From. https://www.verywellmind.com/what-is-active-listening-3024343

SkillsYouNeed. *Barriers to Effective Listening | SkillsYouNeed.* Retrieved From. https://www.skillsyouneed.com/ips/ineffective-listening.html

Mara. (2023). *Active Listening: A Key to Deeper Intimacy and Understanding in Your Relationship.* Retrieved From. https://nyc-couples-therapy.com/active-listen-ing-a-key-to-deeper-intimacy-and-understanding-in-your-relationship/

Klatte, M, Bergstrom, Kristin, and Lachmann, T. (2013). *Does noise affect learning? A short review on noise effects on cognitive performance in children.* Retrieved From. https://www.ncbi.nlm.nih.gov/pmc/articles/PMC3757288/

Dunn, E, PhD, Konrath, S., PhD. (2018). *Dealing with digital distraction.* Retrieved From. https://www.apa.org/news/press/releases/2018/08/digital-distraction

Course Sidekick. *5.2 Barriers to Effective Listening | Communication Studies.* Retrieved From. https://www.coursesidekick.com/communications/study-guides/atd-pima-communication/5-2-barriers-to-effective-listening

Roy, Tamal. (2023). *How can mindful breathing help you actively listen and improve team performance.* Retrieved From. https://www.linkedin.com/advice/3/how-can-mindful-breathing-help-you-actively-listen

Psychology & Mental Health | Britannica. *The psychology of communication.* Retrieved From. https://www.britannica.com/topic/communication/The-psychology-of-communication

Kursk, Lauren M. (2023). *The Power of Words: How Word Choice Impacts Communication and Relationships.* Retrieved From. https://www.linkedin.com/pulse/power-words-how-word-choice-impacts-communication-lauren-marie-kutsko

BetterExplained. *Brevity Is Beautiful.* Retrieved From. https://betterexplained.com/articles/brevity-is-beautiful/

Elharony, Amr. (2023). *The Silence Between the Notes: The Role of Pauses in Effective Communication.* Retrieved From. https://www.linkedin.com/pulse/silence-between-notes-role-pauses-effective-amr-elharony

Fryer, Bronwyn. (2003). *Storytelling That Moves People.* Retrieved From. https://hbr.org/2003/06/storytelling-that-moves-people

SkillsYouNeed. *Assertiveness - Tips & Techniques.* Retrieved From. https://www.skillsyouneed.com/ps/assertiveness-techniques.html

Schmitz, T. (2016). *The Importance of Emotional Awareness in Communication.* Retrieved From. https://www.conovercompany.com/the-importance-of-emotional-awareness-in-communication/

Communispond. *Effective Communication: the Power of Metaphor.* Retrieved From. https://communispond.com/insights/blog/415/effective-communication-the-power-of-metaphor/

Spencer, L. (2022). *20+ Effective Public Speaking Skills & Techniques to Master.* Retrieved From. https://business.tutsplus.com/tutorials/effective-public-speaking-skills-techniques--cms-30848

Esposito, J., MSW. *Conquering Stage Fright.* Retrieved From. https://adaa.org/understanding-anxiety/social-anxiety-disorder/treatment/conquering-stage-fright

Anonymous. *Principles of Persuasion | Professional Communications.* Retrieved From.

https://courses.lumenlearning.com/suny-mcc-businesscommunication/chapter/14-2-principles-of-persuasion/

Martin Chloe. (2022). *Importance of Body Language in Presentations (+ Good & Bad Examples)*. Retrieved From. https://blog.moderngov.com/importance-of-body-language-in-presentations-good-bad-examples

Gratis, Brandi. (2022). *Overcoming cultural barriers to communication.* Retrieved From. https://nulab.com/learn/collaboration/overcoming-cultural-barriers-communication/

Stevenson University Online. *How Cultural Awareness Promotes Effective Communication.* Retrieved From. https://www.stevenson.edu/online/about-us/news/cultural-awareness-effective-communication/

Forbes Councils Member | Forbes. (2022). *Leading A Global Team? Eight Ways To Respect Cultural Differences.* Retrieved From. https://www.forbes.com/sites/theyec/2022/06/01/leading-a-global-team-eight-ways-to-respect-cultural-differences/

Barot, Hrideep | Frantically Speaking. *11 Effective Communication Strategies To Resolve Conflict.* Retrieved From. https://franticallyspeaking.com/11-effective-communication-strategies-to-resolve-conflict/

Harlem World Magazine. *The Importance Of Active Listening In Conflict Management at the Workplace.* Retrieved From. https://www.harlemworldmagazine.com/the-importance-of-active-listening-in-conflict-management-at-the-workplace/

Baer, Mark B, Esq. | Psychology Today. (2017). *Empathy Is the Key to Conflict Resolution or Management.* Retrieved From: https://www.psychologytoday.com/us/blog/empathy-and-relationships/201702/empathy-is-the-key-conflict-resolution-or-management

Corliss, Julie | Harvard.edu. (2021). *The art of a heartfelt apology.* Retrieved From. https://www.health.harvard.edu/blog/the-art-of-a-heartfelt-apology-2021041322366

Hauser, Philipp. *Social Cues | Definition, Types & Examples.* Retrieved From. https://study.com/learn/lesson/social-cues-types-examples.html

Diners, Jason | Inc. (2015). *7 Conversational Tricks to Appear More Confident.* Retrieved From. https://www.inc.com/jayson-demers/7-conversational-tricks-to-appear-more-confident.html

Spokeo | Quora. *How to go past small talk and get into deeper conversations.* Retrieved From. https://www.quora.com/How-do-you-go-past-small-talk-and-get-into-deeper-conversations

Dushime, Eric. (2023). *Building Better Relationships Through Effective Communica-*

tion: Skills and Tips. Retrieved From: https://www.linkedin.com/pulse/building-better-relationships-through-effective-skills-immanuel

Heibutzki, Ralph | Career Advancement. (2021) *Effective Communication in Career Advancement.* Retrieved From. https://work.chron.com/effective-communication-career-advancement-26019.html

Indeed Editorial Team | Indeed. (2022). *8 Effective Networking Strategies for Professionals.* Retrieved From. https://www.indeed.com/career-advice/career-development/networking-strategies

Harrison, Kim. (2020). *Mastering Persuasive Communication at Work: Four Steps to Influence and Success.* Retrieved From. https://cuttingedgepr.com/articles/four-steps-persuasive-communication-work/

Hunt, Jaime | Forbes Communications Council. (2022). *How To Give And Receive Feedback To Strengthen Your Work.* Retrieved From. https://www.forbes.com/sites/forbescommunicationscouncil/2022/01/11/how-to-give-and-receive-feedback-to-strengthen-your-work/

James, Colin | The Colin James Method. (2021). *Why Communication Skills Development Are A Lifelong Learning Journey.* Retrieved From. https://colinjamesmethod.com/communication-skills-development-is-lifelong-learning/

Sharp Emerson, Mary. (2021). *8 Ways You Can Improve Your Communication Skills.* Retrieved From. https://professional.dce.harvard.edu/blog/8-ways-you-can-improve-your-communication-skills/

Novak, David R. (2020). *Self-Assessing Communication.* Retrieved From https://davidrnovak.com/writing/article/2020/03/self-assessing-communication

The Role Of Technology In The Evolution Of Communication https://www.forbes.com/sites/solrogers/2019/10/15/the-role-of-technology-in-the-evolution-of-communication/

Made in United States
Orlando, FL
26 January 2024

42954212R00098